A Dolphin Summer

A DOLPHIN

SUMMER

Gerard Gormley

TAPLINGER PUBLISHING COMPANY, NEW YORK

Published in 1985 by
Taplinger Publishing Co, Inc.
New York, New York

Copyright 1985 by Gerard Gormley
All rights reserved
Published in the United States of America

Library of Congress Cataloging in Publication Data
Gormley, Gerard.
  A dolphin summer.

  Includes index.
  1. Atlantic white-sided dolphin. I. Title.
QL737.C432G68   1985   599.5'3   84-26841
              ISBN 0-8008-2264-1

To Herb Kenny,
who always keeps the faith.

Acknowledgments

For his thoughtful critique and encouragement, my very special thanks to Dr. George Nichols, Jr., president of The Ocean Research & Education Society, Inc., Gloucester, Massachusetts.

Thanks also to Scott Mercer of New England Whale Watch, Inc., for his continued hospitality at sea and for the many observations of cetacean behavior he has passed along to me.

For his critique of the first draft, and for the reference material he provided, I'm grateful to Dr. Steven Katona, College of the Atlantic, Bar Harbor, Maine.

Finally, my thanks to Charlotte Spintig for her able assistance at the keyboard.

Foreword

Although I have used a narrative as a framework, this book is based on personal and secondhand observations and on relevant scientific literature. I have done my best to avoid speculation. Still, where a species' natural history is poorly understood, I indulge myself as needed to weave my story, sometimes borrowing from the behavior of captive animals.

The book's principal character is a female Atlantic white-sided dolphin. Although these animals are common in the western North Atlantic, surprisingly little has been written about them. When asked why I chose one as the subject of my book, my response is simple. They are beautiful, exciting animals.

Gerard Gormley
October 1984

Contents

One

LATE APRIL, YET ONLY RECENTLY has New England
snapped the bonds of winter. Fishermen huddle in
wheelhouses, warming their hands around steaming
mugs as chugging draggers breast the darkness. This
night, though, some seamen brave the cold to gaze
above them, for the sky is a blizzard of stars and the
heavens not far above each vessel's masthead light.

Three hundred miles east of Cape Ann, dawn is extending a slate blue line across the sea. Heading southwesterly over the continental slope, forty-two Atlantic
white-sided dolphins slip with facile grace through the
long ocean swells. Though the sea here is warmed by
the Gulf Stream, the air is crisp, and the dolphins' exhalations raise plumes of mist that fall away behind them.

The air above the dolphins is hushed, but the sea below them quivers with sound; distant hammer blows of
sperm whales probing great dark depths in search of
squid, the squeaks and grunts of countless fishes, deep
moaning calls of fin whales, murmurings of a far-off

1

submarine rock slide. The dolphins analyze each sound, while adding their own click-whistle chorus to the sea's never ending concert.

This is a reproductive herd comprising seven mature males, twenty-seven mature females, and nine yearlings. Most of the mature animals have been together for a good part of their adult lives. The herd is divided into groups of three to five individuals who prefer each other's close company, and those in each group swim and breathe as one. Overall is a sense of herd rhythm, although within a roughly chevron-shaped formation, the various groups often shift positions.

Swimming just below the surface, the dolphins raise smooth hillocks on the calm sea as thin sheaths of water, held together by surface tension, swell to their passage. The satin surface is torn only by an occasional dorsal fin and when the dolphins breathe, by small puffs of spray. From a distance, they convey the impression of a moving tidal rip, a group of mysterious mounds racing along the surface. This swimming style is typical of the species at speeds below ten knots, but at higher speeds, the animals usually "porpoise" (leap from the water while breathing) in order to save energy.[1] For no apparent reason save exuberance, they often leap twenty feet out of the water, performing spins and somersaults. Because of their spectacular aerobatics, Newfoundlanders dubbed them "jumpers."

Stars faded in the day's advancing light. For a time, sea and sky flowed together in one unbroken sweep of purple, then sunrise flared at the ocean's rim and the placid surface gleamed like molten gold.

A sudden disruption broke the fluid motion of the herd. Two females had fallen behind. One was arching her body as though in convulsions. The other nuzzled her, whistled, nuzzled again. The rest of the dolphins doubled back and surrounded the two females. Vocalization shifted to ultrasound, audible over shorter distances and less likely to attract predators while the herd slowed its pace to accommodate the gravid female.

The sun cleared the horizon. Now all could see as well as echo-sense that the female had reached full term.[2] Her once smoothly rounded belly was distorting and rippling as the baby positioned itself for the birthing. Still swimming, even at the height of her labor, she paused every few minutes to arch her body. At one point she mewed briefly, perhaps in pain, but other than that, was silent. At length, her genital slit dilated and small flukes appeared, tightly curled to ease their exit. The other dolphins moved close to watch the birthing.

The baby had spent eleven months inside her mother's womb at a temperature of 96 degrees. To be ejected from her snug little pouch into a vast world of 60-degree water is one of nature's cruel shocks.

A puff of blood, a stinging pain as the umbilical cord parted at her navel. Then she was pushed to the surface by her mother's companion and supported while she took her first breath.[3] Lacking the blanket of insulating blubber that would come with time, she trembled violently, but specialized vascular networks soon minimized the loss of body heat. Bundles of veins surrounding key arteries absorbed and returned to her body core much of the heat that would otherwise be lost through her extremities. Within minutes, her shivering subsided.[4]

Her mother entered a second, milder stage of labor, and expelled the afterbirth. Like a large dismembered jellyfish, the crimson and purple placenta floated to the surface and drifted away as the dolphins moved on. (Not once during labor or birthing had mother or group come to a full stop.) A scant fifty yards behind them, the dorsal fin of a shark parted the silken surface, and the placenta disappeared in a sudden boil. Swimming in overlapping circles and making loud snapping sounds, three scar-laced elders dropped behind, but the shark—a large one, judging by its acoustic image—maintained its distance, and the herd moved on without incident, maintaining a slow pace while the mother examined her baby.

Except for the flabby curl of her dorsal fin and flukes, which would straighten and stiffen in a matter of hours, the baby was a small replica of the adults. Her back, flippers, flukes, and the top of her head were black. Her undersides and lower jaw were white. Black patches encircled her eyes and genital slit. Her sides were gray except for long narrow bands of white extending from below the dorsal fin to the flare of her flukes. Just above her white side patches were long streaks of yellow and tan. Viewed from the side, her peducle appeared thick and sausagelike all the way to her flukes, but was tapered when viewed from above. She was three feet long, more than a third her mother's length.

The mother looked her baby over carefully, then

4

pressed her beak against various parts of the little one's body, listening to her vital signs. Apparently satisfied as to the health of her newborn, she increased her swimming pace.

Instinctively hugging her mother's flank, the baby found that the mother's pressure field carried her along as if by an invisible tether. Even when the herd increased speed to about eight knots, she was able, with minimal use of her flukes, to keep up and remain in her mother's pressure field through fairly tight turns.[5]

The adults vocalized continually as they swam. Their high-pitched whistles and chirps, their buzzes and clicks were all familiar to the baby, for during much of her time in the womb she had been conscious of her mother making such sounds. Also familiar, but much louder than before, were the lower-frequency sounds made by various other creatures of the sea. Her acutely sensitive hearing canals seemed bombarded with grunts, booms, moans, cackles—all manner of raucous sounds—coming from the darkness below her.

In time, she would learn to tune out most of these lower-frequency sounds, as the adults did. For a while, though, she would find this world into which she had been plunged a noisy, frightening place.

A nine-foot blue shark materialized out of the dusky depths on the herd's left. Rolling white-rimmed eyes the size of large sand dollars, the slender sickle-tailed animal looked the dolphins over, then doubled back on itself and fell in behind the herd. It swam there for a while, then made a slow sweep under the dolphins, perhaps checking out the baby, and took up a position to the right of the herd.

Ultramarine above and silvery white below, the shark had only to move about twenty feet farther away to disappear behind the blue veil of distance. It did so now and again, with impressive speed, as though to remind the dolphins how agile it could be, should the need arise. Its maneuvers were likely born of caution, for it was greatly outnumbered.

The baby was closely flanked by two adults: her mother on the left and another female on the right. The baby had noted the second female's presence since birth. It was she who helped the little one to the surface for her first breath, and she has been a constant companion ever since.

The blue shark had been swimming on the friend's side of the herd. As the shark again moved into visible range, the friend turned toward it and emitted a loud, sharp *crack*. The shark recoiled from the sound as though physically struck, then with a single whiplike thrust of its caudal fin, dissolved into the deep blue twilight of depth and distance. The friend returned to her place beside the baby.

The baby heard the friend's heartbeat quicken just before she turned toward the shark, but now that the animal was gone, her pulse once again sounded normal. While in the womb, she had often heard her mother's heartbeat accelerate, and she had received flashes of fear through some complex biochemical link to the mother's emotional states.

Now she associated rapid heartbeats with sharks, at

least those that ventured close to the herd, and would be wary of them.

While the friend was away, the baby felt exposed and vulnerable. Now that she again had her mother on one side and their friend on the other, she was glad. The presence of the two adults comforted her, made the sea seem less immense.

The continual proximity of mother and friend is vital to the little one's survival. Their combined pressure fields carry the baby along with minimal effort on her part, and the moving enclosure formed by their large bodies is reminiscent of the cozy quarters she so long enjoyed within her mother's womb. Without this sense of security, she would probably succumb within five or six years to perforated ulcers or other stress-induced disorders, for danger is ever present in her environment.[6] Even if she survived years of stress without physical malfunctions, she would probably be too neurotic to care properly for her own babies. Thus, the security granted each baby by its mother and "nanny" is, in the long term, vital to the survival of the species.

Hunger gurgled loudly in the baby's stomach, and she mewed her discomfort. The mother rolled over and swam on her side. Association, assisted by the mother's black genital patch, led the baby to nuzzle the portal to the warm sanctuary that had nurtured her for so many months. Two mammary slits straddled the mother's cloacal opening. When the baby pressed her beak against one of the slits, it spurted yellow milk having the consistency of yogurt, and tasting of fish. Fifty percent fat and rich in protein, phosphorous, and calcium, the milk would quickly thicken the baby's warming blanket of blubber and stimulate rapid growth of bones and muscles.

Her first attempts at nursing were clumsy ones; much of the milk dribbled from her mouth. Globules of congealed fat streamed away behind her, bobbing like solid bubbles in the herd's wake. She vented her hunger and frustration with little, mewlike squeals, but continued to nurse, though she swallowed much seawater with her milk. [7]

As though they had been waiting for this precise moment, hundreds of tiny fish began following the dolphins, snatching up every morsel of fat that spewed from the baby's mouth. The little fish—fingerlings of many different species—soon numbered in the thousands, many of them swarming around the baby's head, some even darting partway into her mouth as demand began to exceed supply. Not a molecule was wasted. The fats and proteins of the fishes that went into the making of the milk would nourish other fish that might in turn feed dolphins.

Through trial and error, the baby learned to curl the sides of her tongue against the roof of her mouth, forming a channel that guided the milk into her throat. She still ingested some seawater along with the milk, but her progress could be measured by the diminishing number of fishes following her. Finally, she burped a couple of bubbles of contentment and abandoned the mammary slit.

Since some hours before the baby's birth, long oceanic swells had been running smooth and silent out of the southeast, and the swimming was easy. Now, with the sun well clear of the horizon, the wind freshened from the northwest, bunching the surface into short, choppy waves that made breathing difficult for the baby. Soon the waves curled high, breaking white, and she frequently took water into her blowhole. Inner check valves prevented the water from reaching her trachea, but she had to clear her blowhole with loud sneezelike chuffs.

Mother and nanny surfaced with their bodies broadside to the wind, forming a breakwater that enabled the baby to breathe more easily. The rest of the dolphins seemed to understand, and changed course slightly to accommodate the maternal group.

They moved southwesterly until the sun was nearly overhead; then the wind slackened, and the herd formed a slow tight circle, moving counterclockwise. As the dolphins circled, each closed the left eye, but kept the right eye open. After circling for ten or fifteen minutes, they made an S-turn and reversed direction, this time with the right eye closed and the left eye open. Already, the little female was learning to observe and mimic every action of mother and friend. She had no idea why she should swim with one eye closed, but she did so.[8]

Someday she will understand that she is resting in halves. She may even find herself beginning to dream in one side of her brain while the other side remains fully aware of her surroundings. When the sleep circle is reversed and she changes eye states, a dream might stop as suddenly as it began and be replaced a few minutes later by a different dream.

The dreams of one so young would probably be fetal recollections, perhaps swimming or suckling dreams that recurred while she was in the womb. Such dreams could serve to exercise her muscles and prepare her for life outside her mother's body.

After an hour or so, the sleep circle dissolved and the dolphins milled about lazily, clicking and whistling, some of the females nursing yearlings who were twice the newborn female's size. The groups intermingled, and a few males made some halfhearted attempts at coitus with the females. At a leisurely pace, one group comprising three heavily scarred elders set off toward the southwest. The others followed.

This habit of alternating eye states while moving in sleep circles has been observed in several species of cetacea. It appears that the eyes facing outward from the circle are always open, as though the animals are remaining watchful. That they are literally watching for danger is doubtful. Despite their excellent vision, turbidity limits visibility in the sea to a hundred feet on average, a short sprint for any swift predator. Thus, vision is of secondary importance to the survival of cetaceans. Hearing is their primary sense, and survival would best be served if their sense of hearing remained active while they "slept." Even more important, they must remain at least partially conscious in order to breathe, for their respiration is voluntary, not spontaneous. This guards against accidental inhalation while their blowholes are submerged.

Accordingly, the changes in eye state may merely reflect a transfer of overall sensory control from one side of the brain to the other. Of course, this presupposes complete interchangeability of the two brain hemispheres, whereby a cetacean could sleep and dream in one side of its brain while remaining conscious in the other. By alternating hemispheric states, the animal could essentially sleep in halves. It might do this while circling, moving in a straight line, or simply hovering below the surface and rising for air as needed.

Such interchangeability may be difficult for many of us to accept, specialized as our cerebral hemispheres are, but early humans may have possessed such ability. The expressions "sleeping with one eye open" and "keeping an eye peeled" may stem from prehistoric times, when our ancestors could not afford to lose consciousness, for fear of falling out of the trees in which they slept or being surprised by predators. After we developed into literate beings, our cephalic hemispheres may have become specialized in processing conscious and subconscious functions.

Hemispheric specialization may be a result of cultural, rather than biological, evolution. For example, the Japanese language so strongly patterns the brains of those who speak it that they process most sounds on the opposite side of the brain from that used by Westerners. Tadanobu Tsunoda of Tokyo Medical and Dental University believes that the Japanese process emotion in the dominant hemisphere, again the opposite of Westerners. He speculates that logic and emotions are not hemispherically separated in the Japanese brain, but are probably both functions of the same verbal hemisphere.

For the rest of that day the herd continued to swim generally toward the southwest, changing direction as hunger and whim dictated.

About midafternoon, the leaders turned abruptly south and began clicking steadily. Soon all the dolphins were spreading out across a wide front, buzzing as they went. Minutes later they closed on a large school of herring, thousands of silvery fish, so densely packed and single-minded in their movements that they flowed through the sea like a gleaming whale. As the dolphins approached, the fish nearest them darted back and forth, causing the rear of the school to sweep like the tail of a single large animal.

The herd went deep, then assumed the shape of a crescent and came up under the school, forcing it to the surface.[9] Circling on their sides, the dolphins used their flashing white underbellies to frighten and contain the herring. Then the various groups took turns going in to feed, while the rest continued circling.

When it came time for her mother and nanny to feed, the baby found herself suddenly immersed in silvery bodies. The frightened fish pelted against her face and sides in such overwhelming numbers that she panicked and darted to the surface. All around her, fish were so tightly packed that many were leaping out of the water in an effort to escape the hunters. She squealed in fright and thrust herself ahead, skittering across the solid mass of bodies toward open water.

Her mother and friend surfaced beside her and began snatching fish out of the air, catching them head first and swallowing them whole. As they fed at their leisure, the baby shook off her fear and mimicked the adults. An eight-inch herring leaped toward her, and she caught it, but the fish squirted out from between her toothless gums and melted back into the writhing mass of silver bodies. No loss. It is doubtful that she could have eaten the fish. She was simply following her mother's example, perhaps thinking this a pleasant game.

As the baby reared back at the surface, a largely undiscovered aspect of her vision came into play. Her eyes were placed so far back on her head that they operated independently for the most part, giving her little or no depth perception. Within a narrow field of view below her head, however, she could focus both eyes on the same object and gain a good idea of its distance. She had noticed this to some degree underwater, but now, in the longer range visibility of air, her field of depth perception became dramatically clear.

As she bobbed at the surface, using her newfound binocular vision, a movement east of the school caught her attention. Two fin tips slashed the surface, heading directly toward her at astonishing speed. In the second or so that it took her to comprehend what she was seeing, the fins had closed from two hundred feet away to about half that distance.

Mother and friend spotted the fins a moment after the baby did. They paused long enough to sound sharp thwacks against the surface with their flukes, then with the suckling between them, they thrust their way down through the tightly packed fish into clear water twenty feet below. As they headed down, the two females emitted loud cracks, a traditional danger signal among many species of cetacea.

At a depth of fifty feet, they leveled off and looked up. The scene above was one of massacre. The two fins they had seen streaking along the surface were the high dorsal and caudal fins of a ten-foot broadbill swordfish, which had slammed into the herring school at forty knots, slashing its three-foot sword from side to side like a saber. The swift attack had cut a wide swath through the school, leaving the surface littered with dead and injured herring. Free of the encircling dolphins, who had scattered when the warning was sounded, the main body of the herring school sought safety in the depths. The swordfish began scooping fish into its toothless maw, but lost most of the smaller ones to a flock of kittiwakes that dropped from the sky. The birds had followed the broadbill, reading the signs in the sea like a guidebook.

When the dolphins regrouped a few hundred yards to the south, blood was oozing from the side of a young male who apparently failed to get out of the way in time. The broadbill's sword had ripped an eight-inch gash in the dolphin's side, penetrating his inch-thick blubber, but fortunately for him, merely grazing the muscle tissue. Even as the other dolphins milled around, tasting his blood (they have little or no sense of smell) and clicking among themselves, blubber oozed into the wound and stopped the bleeding.[10]

14

He would survive, but the long scar would be with him for life.

In the slope waters between the continental shelf and the Gulf Stream, the water temperature near the surface seldom drops much below 60 degrees Fahrenheit. Here, the dolphins often encounter large swordfish and marlin. These animals prey only on smaller fishes, never on cetaceans, but they attack their prey with such speed and wild abandon that no creature in their path is safe. The swords of broadbills and marlin have been found embedded in the bodies of whales. Even boats are occasionally rammed and run through.

Dolphins are usually able to avoid injuries such as the one suffered by the young male. In the noisy confusion of a hunt, though, with thousands of fishes emitting frightened bladder squeaks and deafening the dolphins to what lies beyond the school, such accidents do happen. Sometimes they are fatal.

Atlantic white-sided dolphins appear to spend most of the winter in the continental slope waters, ranging as far north as Sable Island and as far south as the New York Bight. The middle-depths of the slope waters constitute the major winter range for most of their food fish. This belt of temperate water may also be important to the well-being of babies born in the earlier part of the birthing season, for they are not arctic creatures, and the early arrivals may have to nurse for several weeks before their blubber becomes thick enough to insulate them from the cold upwellings around the fishing banks nearer the coast.[11]

Late in the afternoon, as the adults turned west, pursuing a school of mackerel, the baby dolphin noticed certain changes taking place in her environment. Cold upwellings from the depths were beginning to chill her. The water tasted brinier and more fishlike than before. The sounds reaching her from the darkness below were louder and more varied.

She heard swishing and creaking sounds emanating from large surface swimmers that she would come to recognize as fishing vessels. These things belched smoke, and when she raised her head clear of the water, she heard strange callings. One of the vessels passed close enough for her to see upright creatures moving about with strangely jerky motions, paying out a huge net while the seiner moved in a great foamy, bubbling circle.

The leaders quickly concluded the hunt. They circled south, avoiding the purse seiner and heading back into the slope waters. They had strayed over the edge of the continental shelf, the northeastern periphery of the vast submarine mesa known as Browns Bank, one of the area's major fisheries. The water over Browns Bank was too cold for the little female and other babies yet to come, so the herd moved farther offshore. As their circle carried them back over the continental slope, the baby felt the water warming.

The dolphins would remain far offshore for several more weeks, moving parallel to the continental shelf along a ragged line running northeast to southwest. As the great schools of fish moved westerly on their spring migrations to inshore waters, the dolphins would have good hunting.

Huge, oblate, blood red, the sun slipped behind the western horizon. The wind died, and the sea settled into a glassy twilight hush that betrayed any surface activity, however minor or carefully conducted. From hundreds of yards away, the slightest plip of a small fish snatching tidbits from the surface was audible to the dolphins. The lacy "finning" of menhaden schools, the fine rippling passage of herring, the slow rolling boil of mackerel—all were detectable in the flat calm. As the dolphins pursued the schools, the smooth swells of their head waves zigged this way and that along the surface.

Able to hear the fishes' surface feeding sounds, the dolphins could stalk each school in silence, but the close pursuit and capture of individual fish required active echolocation, for the dolphins' eyes are too far back on their heads for them to see directly ahead of their beaks.[12] Each hunt began as a silent stalk well below the surface and then, as the dolphins sonared and closed for the kill, climaxed in an explosion of leaping fish. The dolphins had the schools all to themselves, and the hunting was easy. They moved from school to school, triggering finny eruptions on the placid surface as they enjoyed a smorgasbord of menhaden, herring, mackerel, alewives, and shad.

As darkness flowed across the sea and the surface concentration of plankton increased, more and more fish schools swept through the area. Too full to eat so much as a sardine, the dolphins circled and napped while the eaters of plankton fed all around them.

On this, the baby dolphin's first night in the sea, she

17

was terrified. She could not see anything, even her mother, though her flipper was brushing that reassuring side. The baby's only consolations were her mother's touch and the clicking, whistling sounds of the herd. Their calls gave her a sense of belonging and made the blackness tolerable.

A full moon rose, as large as the setting sun and nearly as red, silhouetting the circling dolphins in a swath of reflected amber light. As the moon ascended, it paled to gold, then became such a brilliant white that the calm sea gleamed like liquid silver.

The baby derived some comfort from the moonlight. Later that year, when she started developing her active echolocation abilities, light and darkness would make little difference to her peace of mind. Until then, she would hear in the passive sense only, and the nights would continue to frighten her. Watching the moon, a reassuring light, with her open eye, she managed to relax a bit and rest.

About thirty minutes later, a loud whoosh brought the baby wide awake. The adult dolphins simply continued circling, as though they heard nothing. Another whoosh came to her, louder than the first! A column of mist rose twenty feet in the air, forming a pale rainbow in the moonlight as a monstrous black form whispered swiftly through the water a scant fifty feet from the dolphins' sleep circle. Other spouts blossomed abruptly in the moonlight, and three more gigantic backs topped by curved dorsal fins sped slickly, quietly past the dolphins. The herd slumbered on, seemingly oblivious to the passing giants.

Finback whales, their smaller minke cousins, and

humpback whales were feeding on fish and krill. The whales frightened the suckling when they passed near, though she could see only the upper portions of their bodies breaking the surface. Her fear was moderated by the normal pace of her mother's heartbeat, but she remained edgy. Then for two hours the dolphins napped as an overcast moved in, drawing a dark blanket over the moon.

Borne on the currents, a vast cloud of phosphorescent plankton came drifting along. Soon the spoutings of the whales showed traces of ghostly blue-green fire. The sea slid from their backs in glowing sheets. Fish schools pursued by the whales darted and weaved like runaway constellations. The whales ate their fill, then in twos and threes settled down to rest. All was quiet for nearly an hour.

A loud grunt brought the baby dolphin wide awake, just as the calm surface shattered into glowing fragments and a humpback soared clear of the water. He floated in the air for a moment, a monstrous shadow silhouetted against the overcast, glowing rivers cascading from his flippers and flanks. Then, leaning to one side, he thundered back into the sea. The splash of his reentry formed a bejeweled coronet twenty feet high, that dazzled on the air.

As the outrushing wave raised by the whale's breach lifted the dolphins and set them down again, they roused from their slumber and reared back at the surface to watch.

Again and again the humpback hurled himself out of the sea, harnessing lightning, summoning thunder. Some of his leaps were vertical. Other times, he breached at an angle, and while airborne, performed barrel rolls. Forty-two times he breached, with scarcely a minute's pause between leaps. Each breach illuminated the area like an eruption of pale blue-green lava. Other humpbacks slapped their flippers against the water, raising great fountains of light. The white-sides bobbed at the surface, watching, and the little female's eyes were wide with wonder.

As suddenly as it began, the breaching stopped and the whales returned to their naps. As the white-sides moved among the sleeping leviathans, the baby heard their cavernous drafts of breath, their deep, moaning calls, so powerful that they nearly made her nauseated. An immense bubble of flatulence blooped from beneath one whale and boiled briefly at the surface.

Slumbering on a current, the whales drifted off toward the north. The phosphorescent plankton drifted away, too, and with it the magical sea fire. The dolphins headed southwest. The sea flattened in blackness and dim moonlight, where for a brilliant moment the great whales feeding in the phosphorescent waters had raised a magic show of interchanging light and mammoth motion.

Humpbacks have been observed breaching over a hundred times in rapid succession. They are famous for their spectacular leaps, but breaching has been observed in all species of large whales. Even the normally sluggish right whales are quite acrobatic when the spirit moves them.

What moves whales to expend such tremendous

amounts of energy? They may breach to dislodge parasites or relieve flatulence. Some scientists think males breach to announce territories during mating season. Then again, humpbacks breach year-round, and there is no evidence that breaching is restricted to males.

No one knows for certain why whales breach. All the above reasons, and more, may apply. Perhaps they breach because it feels good. As humans enjoy diving into water, so whales may like leaping into air, feeling sunlight and wind on their sensitive skins. Born into water, moving always through its endless immensity, they must be drawn now and then to make brief visits into that strangely thin medium overhead. Breaching may be play, sheer fun, the high spirits seen in otters on their slides.

Two

OVER THE NEXT FOUR WEEKS, six more females reached full term and bore healthy babies. Each was attended by a friend, who closely monitored the birth and assisted the newborn to the surface for its first breath. The little one, firstborn this year, was excited by the appearance of each new suckling.

One more female remained gravid. On the day she began labor, everything seemed to go badly. A squall swooped down out of the northeast, drawing long tatters of black cloud across the sun and whipping the sea into fifteen-foot waves. The herd descended to a depth of ninety feet to escape the worst of the wave action, but every time they surfaced for air, the laboring female was buffeted by the storm and suffered a great deal of pain.

Her labor was long and arduous, and her whistles of distress continued for hours, attracting half a dozen blue sharks that now followed the family doggedly, driven by their seemingly perpetual hunger.

At last, small flukes extended from the female's ventral slit. The attendant nudged the flukes, and received a twitch response. The baby had survived the labor. Soon the baby's entire tail was protruding, severely restricting the mother's swimming speed and maneuverability. The sharks started to close toward her, but a dozen dolphins came to her defense. Punctuating their buzzing sonar sounds with frequent sharp cracks—a sort of battle cry—the dolphins streaked back to ram the sharks, but the blues were amazingly agile. Maneuvering with their long pectoral fins, the sharks snapped their supple bodies into high-speed U-turns and avoided the attack. By the time the dolphins turned to make another run, the blues had faded into the depths.

Meanwhile, the laboring dolphin had slowed desperately. The umbilical cord was stretched to the breaking point, but holding. The mother expressed her pain and fear with mewlike squeals, then went into convulsions. Blood billowed darkly from her birth canal. The attendant scanned the mother's body with ultrasound, then suddenly bit through the umbilical cord, grasped the baby's flukes in her jaws, and tugged hard. The cloud of blood grew larger, the mother's convulsions more severe. Still, the attendant persisted, tugging at the baby's flukes with strong sideways thrusts of her head.[1]

Finally the baby popped free and dangled limply from the attendant's jaws. Now all could sense what the problem was. The baby's dorsal fin had been erect, not folded safely down to one side, and the cord had tangled around the fin. The newborn's supply of blood and oxygen may have been pinched off for some time.

Immediately, the attendant pushed the baby to the surface and did her best to keep its head above water, but the towering waves were too much for her. The little one was swept away, and precious seconds were lost as the attendant retrieved the limp form and again attempted to start its breathing. The mother struggled weakly to the surface and tried to help, but was tumbled about by the heavy seas.

One of the older males surfaced beside the attendant. He gripped the baby's left flipper in his jaws, while the attendant took hold of the right one. They held the baby as high out of the water as they could, but to no avail. A wave came crashing down on them and tore the baby away. The lifeless form sank slowly into the depths.

The dolphins followed the little corpse down, touching it with their beaks to listen for vital signs, nudging and nipping it, as though trying to wake it. The mother moved among them and pushed her baby back to the surface. Despite her pain, evidenced by the way she squealed each time a wave crashed down on her, she held the small corpse at the surface. Alternately supporting it with her head and grasping it with her jaws, she rode out the storm for another hour at the surface, refusing to let anyone touch her baby. The squall passed, and still she pushed the corpse. The other dolphins surrounded the grieving mother, and slowed their speed to hers.[2]

For three days the mother pushed her baby's corpse, and for most of that time, blood trickled from her ventral slit. The others brought fish to her. She tried to eat, but soon vomited, and a repugnant green slime accompanied the regurgitated fish. A few hours later, the blood issuing from her cloacal opening turned black, and tasted of death. She became feverish. Her mounting body heat was trapped within by her blubber, and the fever raged out of control. Gripped by a growing delirium, she began swimming erratically and had to be guided by the others.

By sunset of that day, the scent of death coming from the mother and her baby's bloated corpse had attracted five blue sharks and three makos, which were following the herd. Danger now threatened the entire group. As the sharks increased in number, their boldness would grow accordingly. Should their number come to equal or exceed that of the dolphins, they might very well attack. Two of the dolphins tried to separate the mother from her dead baby, but she gripped it tightly in her jaws and refused to release it. Tensions began to mount throughout the herd.

By sunrise, three more blue sharks and another mako had joined the trailing pack. The dolphins faced a choice between loyalty to the ill mother and concern for the common good. Again, several adults pressed her to release the baby, but despite her weakened condition, she refused. By now, the baby was a bloated mass of putrefaction. The dolphins milled about aimlessly, apparently trying to decide on a course of action. When the mother pushed ahead, they followed. For the sake of one, they would risk the safety of all.

Because of the sharks, the dolphins had been unable

to hunt for nearly twenty-four hours. Hunger was worsening an already tense situation.

A growing restlessness at the rear of the herd was accompanied by increased vocalization and repeated shifting of swim positions, then suddenly a dozen adults turned and rushed the sharks. Caught by surprise, one mako was rammed so savagely that it sank out of sight, convulsing and bleeding from its anal slit. The other sharks followed it down into darkness. Soon the sounds of ripping flesh rose from the depths. The dolphins nudged the sick female, urging her on, apparently hoping to leave the distracted sharks behind.

The sharks either satisfied their appetites at the expense of the stricken mako, or lost the dolphins' scent trail. An hour passed, and there was no sign of them.

The ill female slipped into a coma and stopped breathing. Her jaws went slack, and the baby's corpse drifted away on the current. Two dolphins moved in immediately to keep the unconscious female afloat. Resting her flippers across their backs and against their dorsal fins, so that her blowhole was well above water, they continued on with the others forming a protective ring around them.

A hundred yards back, a flock of kittiwakes descended on the baby's corpse. Although kittiwakes seldom eat carrion, they nonetheless ripped and tore at the little dolphin. With a hiss, the corpse released its bloating gases, and sank out of sight. Deprived of their meal, the birds paddled about for a time, then took to the air and followed the dolphins.

Until late that afternoon, the dolphins supported the female. Her heart had stopped beating within ten minutes after she lost consciousness; still, they kept her with them, as she had kept her dead baby with her for so long, perhaps hoping that a spark of life remained and could be rekindled. Cetaceans over the ages may have witnessed something akin to what Lyall Watson calls "the Romeo Error." Comrades seemingly dead come suddenly back to life. And so, they wait and wait long after the vital signs are still.[3]

Just before dark, the dolphins stopped and surrounded the corpse, which was still being supported by the two females who had kept it afloat all this time. The body was nuzzled and sonared by all. A dozen dolphins at a time pressed their beaks against the lifeless form, apparently listening for any vital signs that might remain. Two elders slipped their beaks under the flukes and lifted. The entire tail section rose stiffly; rigor mortis was well established.

The dolphins exchanged clicks and whistles for several minutes, then after a final nuzzling examination the two companions released the female. Slowly, the corpse sank out of sight, eventually to be redistributed among many creatures large and small.

The dolphins moved on, their vocalizations now a bit subdued. The female had been with them for many years. Numbered among her survivors were several close friends, two of them the females who supported her for so long after she died.

The little one, this year's firstborn, had trouble comprehending the deaths of mother and baby. In the span of a few days, she had witnessed the full cycle of life, gained some idea of its fragility.

She comforted herself with a helping of milk, then

27

slipped out from between mother and friend long enough to investigate one of the other sucklings swimming nearby. This baby was only five days old, nearly a month younger than she, and still quite fearful. It recoiled from the inquisitive touch of her beak, and hid behind its mother. She tried again with another newborn and met with the same nervous response. Although feeling older and more mature than her neighbors, the little female responded to her mother's whistle and returned to her place in the formation.

Despite the loss of the mother and baby, the herd had realized a net growth of seven. Any year in which the dolphins manage to keep their numbers from dwindling is a good year. Their losses were soon pushed from mind by new demands. As weeks passed, the babies grew sleek and rambunctious on their mothers' rich milk. They would not take solid food for about six months.

The baby dolphin's main window on her world lies beneath her, the only direction in which she can exercise her binocular vision, and the world she sees is one of incessant motion. Virtually everything white-sided dolphins do is carried out on the move, and most of the creatures they encounter are continually in motion. With the bodies of mother and nanny usually blocking her view to either side, the young dolphin's primary visual perspective is like that of a bird skimming the surface in search of food. Below her, a never ending stream of briefly glimpsed images rushes past, sometimes flashing reflected sunlight, more often seen as dusky shapes against the blackest depths.

Heightening the sense of nonstop activity is the broad spectrum of sound coming from all directions, particularly from the ocean floor. Over the continental slope, the variety of life seems endless. Cold, nutrient-rich waters sweep up along the slope from depths of several miles to sustain the lower links of the food chain, while the warming influence of the Gulf Stream to a depth of several hundred fathoms makes the waters habitable year-round for the higher life forms. The result is a diversity of life probably unsurpassed by any area of the world's oceans.

Extending along the outer edge of America's north-eastern continental shelf is a narrow belt of thermally stable water, where the temperature at depths of five to six hundred feet remains between 47 and 53 degrees Fahrenheit year-round. Many schooling fish such as herring and mackerel winter here, populating the thermal belt as far north as Sable Island Bank, and, in the case of the mackerel, at least, as far south as the Carolinas. In this great ribbon of food-rich water, many dolphins and other large predators spend their winters.

In spring, however, the focus of life is turned inshore. The storms of winter churn nutrients from the great depths and mix them into the cold, oxygen-rich waters of the continental shelf, re-enriching such mesa-like bottom formations as Georges, Browns, and Stellwagen Banks. The increased sunlight of spring triggers population explosions among the plankton that feed on the basic nutrients. Hordes of schooling fish head inshore to feed on the plankton, to spawn, or to hunt newly hatched fry and those of the yearlings that opted to spend the winter in shallower waters. Large predators follow the schools, and by mid-May, the Gulf of Maine teems with life.

As the waters over Georges Bank warmed to the low fifties, and the baby dolphins developed sufficient blubber to insulate them, the herd left the continental slope waters and hunted inshore. Myriad legions of mackerel had gone before them, rising from the mid-depths where they spent the winter, flowing shoreward in massive blue-backed schools, each comprising fish of the same age and size.

Most mackerel schools that preceded the dolphins inshore contained yearling tinkers ten to eleven inches long, or fish that are two to four years of age and twelve to fifteen inches in length. The older mackerel, averaging sixteen to seventeen inches, some reaching twenty inches, tend to remain farther offshore all year because they can swim fast enough to hold their own with most predators. These older fish are too large for the dolphins to swallow, so it is with no sense of loss that they leave them behind and follow the younger schools inshore.

The dolphins have seen few herring since their wanderings carried them southwesterly along the slope line, and they will see fewer still as they cross Georges Bank. Although herring are an important part of their diet, the present scarcity causes them no concern. The elders know that herring prefer the waters northeasterly of

Georges Bank, and that they tend to cluster well in-shore during the warmer months, when spawning takes place. There will be herring in abundance once the dolphins reach the inshore waters. Their souther-erly route inshore, meanwhile, will protect the babies from heat loss.

The night's hunts were productive; a late evening feast of short-finned squid and a pre-dawn snack of tinker mackerel. The dolphins wound their swim for-mation into a sleep circle, the females with babies circling near the center, and rested in the day's first light.

While sunrise was still a bright puddle of light on the horizon, the firstborn female heard hammerlike pulses of sound from the south. Soon she could feel the pulses through sensitive nerve endings in her face, like a wash of fine bubbles caressing her skin. The pulses gave way to loud creaking sounds, much like those made by the adult dolphins during a hunt, but more intense and much deeper in pitch.

The dolphins broke off their circling and turned to-ward the sounds. The little female heard the heartbeats of those nearest her accelerate.

A hundred yards away, the sea was parted by what appeared to be a large brown rock with white water cas-cading down its slopes. Sperm whales! Eyes wide, the baby reared back at the surface to focus both eyes on the strange sight. The rocky apparition emitted a mighty whoosh, and a bushy spout rose at a 45 degree angle. What sort of whale had a head like this?

Two more of the strange creatures surfaced and blew, their spouts angled like the first. Building up head

31

waves that looked like breakers approaching a beach, the whales spread out, emitting a screen of ultrasound so intense that the white-sides were thrown into a state of sensory confusion. Unable to hear anything but the bombardment of sound coming from the whales, they milled about aimlessly, acoustically blinded and afraid to swim in any direction.[4]

Perhaps white-sides have only occasional close encounters with sperm whales and do not instinctively fear them. Whatever their reason, the elders apparently showed poor judgment by failing to lead the herd safely clear the moment they first heard the whales. The terrified baby suddenly saw a massive form looming before her. A huge mouth gaped, revealing a toothless upper jaw. Flashing toward her just below the surface was a lower jaw lined with teeth, each the size of her head.

The herd scattered, each group darting off in a different direction. Clapping their great jaws shut on empty water, the sperm whales churned straight through the area where the dolphins had been circling, and continued on toward the northeast.

Most of the dolphins had escaped along the surface leaping between the low rolling waves at nearly thirty knots, maximizing speed and conserving energy by spending as much time in the air as in the water. Having been caught between the whales and the rest of the dolphins, the firstborn baby's group opted to plunge straight down. This proved to be dangerous. As the whales passed overhead, the terrified baby felt herself sucked upward, then slammed downward again by the powerful wash of the great flukes. Tumbled about as though in a strong undertow, the three dolphins managed to escape injury, but the baby would long remember the sight of those sixty-foot silvery gray underbellies passing overhead.

If indeed the sperm whales were bent on eating the dolphins, they seemed unwilling to devote much effort to the hunt. They soon moved out of sight, leaving ragged vapor trails drifting easterly on the morning breeze.

Only here, near the edge of the continental shelf, are the dolphins apt to encounter sperm whales. The cachalots hunt most of their prey in the deep slope waters, diving as far as 3,500 feet in pursuit of their favorite foods, large squid and cuttlefish. They vary their diets with prey caught at or near the surface, and are known to venture west over the outer reaches of Georges Bank.

In addition to squid and cuttlefish, the stomachs of sperm whales have been found to contain seals, sharks up to ten feet in length, fish of various species, and even seabirds. Analyses of sperm whale stomach contents seldom reveal dolphin remains, probably because dolphins are generally so alert and agile. Still, sperm whales can maintain speeds of fifteen to twenty knots for ten minutes or more, and are capable of cooperative hunting techniques, so dolphins are not altogether safe from them.

Sperms are the largest of the toothed whales—the only ones, in fact, to attain the great size of the baleen whales—so it is likely that a mature sperm whale eats whatever it pleases whenever it can catch it. Sperm whales are quick to fight, and very good at it. Even orcas and great white sharks are not likely to provoke them.

As the white-side herd moved westerly over the continental slope, the depth decreased gradually from two miles to a few thousand feet, then shoaled rapidly to a few hundred feet. Soon the dolphins will be echo-sensing the southeast part of Georges Bank, a vast sandbar formed by glacial deposits at the end of the last ice age.

On some parts of Georges Bank, a tall man can wade neck-deep at low tide. I am even told that old photographs show fishermen playing softball two hundred miles out to sea during an unusually low tide. Tree trunks found on the bottom suggest that parts of Georges Bank were once forested islands, although the trees could have been carried there by currents.

Formations like Georges Bank are close enough to the surface for sunlight to reach the bottom and support photosynthesis. This, combined with nutrient-rich upwellings stirred into the Gulf of Maine by winter storms, nurtures vast pastures of algae, the microscopic plants that constitute the sea's most basic life forms. The algae are eaten by herbivorous zooplankton, which in turn are eaten by tiny primary carnivores, which provide food for secondary carnivores, and so on up the pyramid of life to the billions upon billions of fish that make the great banks of the New England coast the world's richest fisheries.

Perhaps for lack of herring and other inshore spawners over Georges Bank, this white-side herd will spend the summer farther inshore. This is not true of all white-sided dolphins. Many are seen over Georges Bank and in the slope waters all summer long. It may be that the various herds spread their hunting ranges throughout the Gulf of Maine to minimize competition.

Groups of white-sides appear to follow the southern contingent of mackerel year-round, migrating along the continental slope to the New York Bight in winter, then back to Georges Bank in the spring. Other groups may follow the northern contingent of mackerel, while still others migrate with the herring and squid.

Georges Bank hosts many large oceanic predators seldom found closer to the coast, so dolphins hunting there may run a higher risk of predation. In order to improve the odds for the babies, some herds may favor the smaller inshore fisheries such as Stellwagen Bank and Jeffreys Ledge.

For these and other reasons yet unknown, migratory habits and food preferences can vary widely among groups within a given species of cetaceans.

As they approached the shallower portions of Georges Bank, the adult dolphins heard mushy, confusing echoes as their pulses glanced off the sandy banks and rocks. Through sensitive nerve endings in their faces, they also felt the turbulence caused by tidal rips rushing between the shoals.

While they were still some distance from the major shoals, there was a marked increase in the volume of sound from the bottom creatures. The snap of combat rattled along the bottom as large lobsters brandished their fighting claws. Like surf rising and receding on a distant beach, the siphon clicks of countless quahogs and scallops intensified, then faded as the dolphins passed over clam beds. Crabs popped like bubbles bursting. Sculpins grunted. With loud crunching sounds, tautogs and wolffish crushed mollusks in their powerful jaws. Booming like pelagic bullfrogs, toadfish announced their territories with deep honking calls. Sea robins squawked and cackled. Frightened school fish squeaked their swim bladders.

Although the little dolphin had no idea what animals were making the various sounds, the acoustical milieu was nonetheless being imprinted on her already large and rapidly growing brain. Each sound was retained in her highly developed acoustic lobes, ready for correlation with visual and sonar identifications as she grew older.

Soon she heard the echolocation sounds of other dolphins, and her group encountered a white-beaked dolphin herd. Although of the same genus as white-sides, white-beaks are larger—up to eleven feet long—and differently patterned. They have white patches around their blowholes and above their flippers. White side-patches extend from ahead of their dorsal fins and curve upward to cover most of their backs, somewhat like the white or gray "saddles" seen on orcas. At a glance, they might well be mistaken for orcas by the way they move, raising their heads high out of the water as they breathe, and sharply arching their backs as they submerge. Some have completely white beaks, but most have the same beak coloration as the white-sides: black on the upper jaws and white on the lower.

The two groups sonared each other, then intermingled. There were three babies in the white-beaked dolphin herd, which numbered only nineteen in all. The adults showed great curiosity about each other's young. The little ones were nuzzled and flipper-patted. Then while the adults examined each other's genitals, the babies cautiously carried out their own introductions.

The firstborn white-side moved among the young strangers, touching them with her beak and flippers. She tried to click and whistle like the adults, but lost so much air with each attempt that she was forced repeatedly to surface and recharge her lungs. A white-beaked baby nipped her tail as she passed, and she chased him. Soon all the babies were darting about, exchanging toothless nips, and the spirit of play spread throughout both herds.

After a few minutes of chase-and-nip, adult males on both sides tried changing the game rules to chase-and-copulate, but the females surfaced and swam on their backs to avoid coitus. A waiting game ensued. Whenever a female rolled over to breathe, she was mobbed by eager males of both species, but few managed even momentary penetration. The females, especially those who had borne babies short weeks ago, were simply not in the mood. The males persisted for ten or fifteen minutes, but to no avail. They and their intended are weightless, and have no limbs for grasping. Cooperation is prerequisite to copulation. Finally, the males gave up their attempts at intercourse, and resorted to roughhouse play among themselves.

Attracted by the noisy frolic, eighty bottlenose dolphins appeared from the east. They paused long enough to circle the group several times, then continued on, heading westerly toward Nantucket.

Soon after the bottlenose dolphins left, thirty pilot

whales come chuffing down out of the north, swimming in a precise chevron formation behind a scarred old male. They approached and mingled easily with the dolphins, but were so large—some of the males nearly twenty feet long—that most of the dolphin babies sought the safety of their mothers' flanks. There were no babies among the pilot whales, but several females appeared gravid.

The firstborn white-side baby was fascinated by the pilot whales' bulbous heads. Encouraged by the normal heartbeat of her mother, she approached one of the smaller whales and blooped a bubble, as she had seen the adult dolphins do when curious or puzzled. Being nearsighted, as most potheads seem to be, the whale sidled close to get a better look at her. She darted back to her mother.

With a flurry of clicks and whistles, the pilot whales regrouped and moved easterly. The two dolphin herds followed, swimming on either side of the whales.

The reason for the pilot whales' sudden departure soon became clear: a school of short-finned squid, pulsing, gliding, now darting deep into twilight as they sensed the approach of predators. The pilot whales and dolphins took several deep breaths, then went into a nearly vertical dive, moving deep under the squid and forcing them back toward the surface. The cetaceans fanned out, forming a great parabolic curve to contain the squid, which the firstborn baby could now see silhouetted against the surface.

Suddenly, the squid split their formation. One group stopped, while another darted away to the left. Ignoring the stationary group, the hunters swung left to follow the other. As the baby passed close by the drifting shapes, she saw that they were merely puffs of "ink," thick as egg whites, each about the size of the squid that had released it. Were the pursuers fishes, they might have attacked the ink decoys, and in so doing, lost sight of the escaping squid.

The dolphins sprinted ahead on either side to contain the squid, while the slower pilot whales began emitting powerful pulses of ultrasound. Stunned, many squid stopped swimming and were easily caught. Others, disoriented, circled aimlessly. The dolphins quickly ate their fill.

The dolphins appeared to be exploiting the potheads, but the relationship is symbiotic. The dolphins help contain the squid, making it easier for the pilot whales to immobilize them. All hunters get their share.[5]

The potheads continued to pursue stragglers from the squid school, but the dolphins headed back across Georges Bank. A short time later, the white-beaked dolphin herd turned westerly toward Cape Cod, while the white-sided dolphins resumed their northwesterly course toward Stellwagen Bank. They were now moving over prime fishing grounds, and the area abounded with draggers and trawlers plying their great nets.

Some of the vessels steamed in circles, paying out purse seines around fish schools that had been detected by sonar or surface feeding activity. As a purse seiner completed its circle, the ends of the seine were joined, the bottom pursed shut, and the net hauled in like a huge onion sack.

Other vessels followed relatively straight courses,

dragging the bottom with otter trawls, long conical nets fitted with vanes that force open the mouths of the nets as they are pulled through the water.

The herd encountered a bachelor group of young white-sided males, who played a dangerous game as they moved through the fishing fleets. Darting into the open mouths of the otter trawls, they fed at their leisure on trapped fish, sometimes remaining inside the nets until the creak of winches and heavy steel cables warned them that the fishermen were starting their back-hauls.

Probably out of concern for the babies, the maternal herd stayed clear of the nets and continued on toward Stellwagen Bank.

Many dolphins, including orcas, become entangled in dragnets and fish traps. Most drown; some are freed; others wind up serving life sentences in oceanaria. Some animals simply blunder into the nets, but many are trapped while seeking an easy meal.

It seems safe to presume that these apparently bright creatures, accustomed to moving freely through a vast fluid world, would sense danger in anything smacking of confinement. What, then, motivates them to risk raiding nets? Laziness, infirmity, advancing age, or incompetence of youth could all play a part at various times. Hunting is hard work, laced with equal parts danger and boredom. For the sake of effortless meals, many predators risk running afoul of us or our machines. Some orcas and smaller dolphins even appear to delight in outsmarting fishermen, but more likely, they view fishermen and their vessels much as they would any major predator that unwittingly herded a free lunch their way.

Of course, many dolphins are netted through no fault of their own, primarily by tuna fishermen who "fish on porpoise" (their term for dolphin) because yellowfin tuna are often found swimming below dolphins. When trapped within the circle of a tuna seine, dolphins could leap over the surface edge, but their natural escape reflex is to dive, and that is how they become entangled. Since the advent of modern purse seiners, millions of dolphins have drowned in tuna nets. Through enforcement, incidental dolphin kills have been greatly reduced, but by no means eliminated.

If these animals are indeed intelligent, why do the survivors of such tragedies not learn from the mistakes of dead friends? Well, it appears that dolphins are doing just that. Karen W. Pryor, author of *Behavior and Learning in Porpoises and Whales* (Naturwissenschaften, 1973), has observed that many dolphins now seem to be adopting new behavior toward tuna seiners. When they spot a tuna vessel, they lie motionless at the surface to make themselves less visible. If pursued, they swim rapidly, staying on the starboard side of the vessel, away from the net deployment machinery. When evasive efforts fail, and they are surrounded by a purse seine, they no longer blunder into the net or try to dive under it, but remain near the center, waiting for the vessel to back down and lower part of the net so that they can swim over it. Once free, they often breach repeatedly, as though celebrating their release.

41

Still, dolphins seldom leap over the tuna nets. Why is it that, despite their other clever adaptations, made over the course of a few generations, they cannot bring themselves to make the easy hurdle over a floating net? How can they be so bright in so many ways, yet so apparently dull when it comes to this?

Sensory confusion may be the reason. Surrounded by a net, dolphins receive sonar echoes from all directions. They may not be able to echo-sense beyond the net because of acoustic scattering, and so may presume that the danger extends far beyond the visible confines of the net. The animals' inherently strong sense of collision avoidance may overload their brains with danger signals, resulting in a partial shutdown of their escape mechanisms.

As the white-side herd left Georges Bank behind and moved farther inshore, the dolphins passed over a series of deep basins, and encountered relatively few fish anywhere near the surface. Swimming steadily for most of one day and night, they traveled the length of Wilkinson Basin and approached the southern reaches of Stellwagen Bank. Within the span of a single morning, the population of fish in the upper waters increased manyfold. As the dolphins reached Stellwagen Bank and turned northerly, large schools of young fish began to appear, and the hunting was good.

The firstborn suckling had had few opportunities to learn how effectively a school formation can protect young fish. By the time she was born, most of the younger fish had begun moving well inshore. The fish that the herd encountered along the continental slope and over Georges Bank were mature, and tended to school only for cooperative hunts. Through their first few years of life, however, many species of fish must travel in schools. The school is their best protection against larger, faster predators, and the little dolphin was about to observe just how dramatically some schools function.

Early morning had come. Scattered puffs of cloud drifted slowly seaward, sharply etched against a mackerel blue sky. The herd was heading northwesterly over Stellwagen Bank, about twenty miles from Provincetown, moving just below the surface in the manner characteristic of white-sided dolphins at speeds below ten knots. Nearby, the long brown backs of three feeding finback whales sliced the surface.

The dolphins had earlier filled their first stomach chambers (like cows and other ruminants, they have four) with young mackerel, so they permitted school after school of fish to pass unmolested. The fish seemed to sense that the dolphins were not hungry, and came quite close.

A large school of tinker mackerel was about thirty feet from the firstborn baby's side of the herd, when a twenty-inch silver hake flashed into view and struck. Quick as a bomb burst, the school expanded outward, creating a large empty space around the silver hake. Not a single mackerel had been harmed. The predator circled in apparent sensory confusion, uncertain as to which way it should make its next strike. Meanwhile, the school flowed around it and regrouped a short distance away. There were no signs of panic or disorder

43

among the mackerel. They continued along like a single large organism, swimming parallel to the dolphins' course, as though awaiting the hake's next move.

Next, the silver hake tried a slow stalking maneuver, apparently hoping to approach close enough to pick off one of the mackerel at the rear of the school. When the hake reached a point about six feet away, the school suddenly split into two parts, which flowed like a fountain around the predator and rejoined behind it. The hake reversed direction and tried another stalk, but the school again split and flowed around behind it.

Frustrated, the hake whipped around and launched itself toward the school with the speed of an arrow leaving a bow. It seemed certain that at least one mackerel would be taken, but again the school expanded like a bomb burst, and the hake was left circling aimlessly, snapping at empty water while the school gradually regrouped at a safe distance.

A dozen more silver hake happened along, and all joined forces to form a hunting school. The group attack was successful. Killing or maiming twice as many mackerel as they could eat, the hake soon satisfied their voracious appetites, and left the area. Numbering about sixty less than before, the mackerel school continued on.

A dozen wounded mackerel were left behind, flipping about at the surface. The firstborn dolphin baby strayed from her mother's side long enough to investigate them, and was nearly struck by a gannet's long sharp beak as the goose-size bird plunged from a height of eighty feet to gobble up the disabled fish. The frightened dolphin darted back to her mother, and received a nip on the flipper as punishment for her carelessness.

Until recently, the schooling behavior of fish was poorly understood. Laboratory investigations conducted by Brian L. Partridge and colleagues in Aberdeen Scotland, have shed light on just how sophisticated the survival tactics of a fish school can be. In a paper published in the June 1982 issue of *Scientific American*, Partridge concluded that fish use a combination of visual and lateral line sensory inputs to maintain school integrity while executing complex maneuvers such as the "fountain effect," a term coined by Geoffry Potts of the Marine Biological Association at Plymouth, England.

One point not covered in Partridge's excellent paper is that schools usually contain fish of the same age and size, which move at about the same speed for a given fin thrust. This plays an important part in the fishes' ability to perform complex high-speed maneuvers without disbanding the school. The relationship between size and swimming speed—larger fish of a given species can swim faster—is also a major reason that members of a species may be obligatory schoolers when young, but merely opportunistic schoolers when they reach adult size and can escape predators on their own.

Three

THE SUNRISE WAS PORTENTOUS. Ribbons of red extended across a slate gray sky. The air was hushed, heavy with latent moisture. An odor of ozone overrode the briny tang of sea. Except for the mounds caused by the dolphins' head waves, the surface was as taut and smooth as an immense satin sheet.

Within an hour after sunrise, the first signs of heavy weather appeared, and the slow rise and fall of long oceanic swells, several hundred feet from crest to crest, made the brooding gray plain of sea appear to breathe. As time passed, the breathing became labored. The long, smooth swells gave way to a nasty chop sweeping out of the northeast, and where sunrise had shone a short while ago, night already seemed to be returning. A spring nor'easter was drawing a black blanket over the Gulf of Maine.

While the storm was still miles away, the dolphins saw lightning forking out of the black lower clouds. Long drum rolls of distant thunder were clearly audible, and between them, a steadily mounting roar. Bobbing high in a wave crest to get a better look, for this was her first experience with electrical storms, the baby observed an onrushing patch of flattened white water. A brief burst of sunlight sent slanting rays below the cloud cover, illuminating a great cascade of sparkling ice particles. The roar grew louder, drowning out warning whistles from the baby's mother and nanny, who had turned back and were rushing toward her.

Seconds before the white water was upon her, the baby dove. All around her, pebble-size hailstones stabbed into the sea to a depth of several feet, leaving slender bubble trails dangling from the surface like countless jellyfish tentacles. The hailstorm swept overhead with a roar so loud that it hurt her sensitive hearing canals. She dove deep, but could not escape the noise. A sudden flash of light was followed instantaneously by the loudest crack she had ever heard. Badly startled by the noise, she lost air and had to surface.

The moment she broke water, hailstones pummeled her head and back, and the stinging forced her to dive again before she had a chance to fill her lungs. She shot back to the surface and gasped for air, only to be driven immediately down again by the battering hailstones.

As she surfaced for the third time, splintered shafts of blue fire began cracking like colossal whips from cloud to sea, shattering her senses with their blinding light and terrifying blasts. Panic-stricken, unable to breathe well enough to remain submerged for more than twenty seconds, she porpoised wildly through the leaping waves, trying to swim beyond the barrage of lightning and hail. Spurred on by her terror, she swam faster than she ever had before, so fast that her mother and nanny had difficulty catching up with her.

By the time the adults reached the little one and managed to wedge her between them, she had already swum clear of the worst hail and lightning. As the storm slowly faded away to the southwest, the baby floated between mother and friend, panting and trembling from her ordeal.[1]

The herd regrouped, but with each crack of thunder from the storm, now nearly a mile away, the sucklings flinched and pressed against their mothers. It had been an ordeal for all of them. The firstborn was so exhausted that she had to take an immediate nap, while still supported between mother and friend.

The herd resumed its northwesterly journey along Stellwagen Bank and about midmorning, encountered a ninety-foot vessel, which hove to and rocked slowly in the swells as the dolphins passed. So many men, women, and children crowded the starboard rail to watch the white-sides, the vessel listed under their weight.

Some of the youngest dolphins tarried a bit at the surface, rolling slightly to one side as they swam, the better to study the vessel and its riders. The firstborn baby had never seen so many humans aboard one vessel. She observed them waving their tentacles and holding black cylinders in front of their eyes. Many voices were audible, but one was much louder than the rest. It bellowed across the water as loudly as the call of a whale, but was staccato, rather than smoothly drawn out, and lacked the musical quality of a whale's voice.

As the herd reached its closest point of approach, the little dolphin could see that some of the creatures on the vessel were no larger than she. She felt that tug of attraction so often shared by the young of various species. Then the vessel slipped away and the voices faded.

A short time later, the dolphins overtook a solitary right whale, the first they had seen for many months. Unlike the finbacks and minkes, the right whale has no dorsal fin, and its nostrils are so far apart that its exhalations form twin spouts. Its head makes up nearly a third of its thick-set forty-foot length, and the bow-shaped arch of its huge mouth gives the impression that the animal is swimming upside down. Wartlike callosities cover much of the head and chin and, seen from a distance, resemble patches of foam, but at close range they look more like clusters of barnacles.

The right whale was swimming slowly at the surface, filtering all but the tiniest organisms from the sea with its finely meshed baleen, which extended nearly seven feet from the upper jaw. As the dolphins passed, the whale closed its mouth and swallowed with a gulp.

Propeller sounds were heard from the southeast, and the vessel that the dolphins had passed a short while before came into view again, heading swiftly toward the right whale. The amplified voice of an excited naturalist announced to the passengers that this is the first right whale he has sighted in three years. The vessel feathered its screws and glided quietly within a hundred feet of the whale, which continued to surface-feed as cameras and hastily jotted notes entered its solitary presence into the records.

The white-sides left the lumbering whale and its admirers far behind, and continued north.

This lone northern right whale might be pregnant—the females of the species are inclined toward solitude when approaching term—or it could be the sole survivor of an extended family. If the latter, then this whale could very well live out its years without having an opportunity to beget offspring and add to its endangered species' numbers, for the last surviving members of extended right whale families may find it difficult to join other families. For one thing, they are not likely to encounter many of their own kind, when there remain only a few hundred, roaming millions of square miles of ocean, and should they chance to meet up with other groups, they simply may not fit in if the strangers' communications and customs differ substantially from theirs.

If clannishness does indeed play a part in right whale communities, it would help explain why the species has not made any appreciable comeback, even though it has been protected by international agreement since 1937. Gray whales, protected since 1946, have shown an encouraging increase in numbers, perhaps because they migrate en masse and have less sharply defined family distinctions. Even blue whales, despite their low reproductive rate and more recent (1967) reprieve from slaughter, are showing better signs of recovery than the right whales.

Monogamy may be another factor limiting the reproductive rate of certain whale species, for some individuals become reclusive when their mates are killed.

Such factors have not been taken into account by the

International Whaling Commission when establishing kill quotas. When whalers kill enough members of a whale family, they may be sentencing that entire family to extinction. Accordingly, the gross population numbers cited by the IWC—already suspect because the figures come from the whalers—may be even more misleading because they fail to consider counterproductive factors such as clannishness and monogamy.

Almost daily now, the herd was encountering other groups of white-sided dolphins hunting along Stellwagen Bank. Several herds often banded together, the better to contain and control the large schools of fish. Sometimes they were joined by pilot whales or white-beaked dolphins, forming groups that numbered many hundreds of animals. These were exciting times for the little ones, and they frequently ventured from their mothers' sides to play chase-and-nip games with each other.

Except when the white-sides were intermingling with other groups of dolphins, the sucklings were expected to remain within the confines of their herd's formation. Transgressors were punished with mild nips, fluke slaps, or head butts. Punishment was usually meted out by the mothers, but if a baby's mother was not nearby at the time a transgression occurred, the nearest adult was likely to butt the little one back into line. While the herd was on the move, the adults maintained a protective ring around the young ones, sometimes, if there were sharks in the vicinity, extending the ring below them in a bowl-shaped formation.

51

Almost daily, the firstborn baby felt her strength and speed increasing. For short distances, at least, she could now swim nearly as fast as the adults, yet she had much to learn about the art of maneuvering, and often suffered painful collisions with other sucklings.

Like a fledgling bird testing its newfound powers of flight, she often sought out a reasonably open space in the herd's formation, and practiced the nuances of flipper and fluke control. The herd's cruising speed was usually at least six knots, sufficiently fast for a slight countertwist of her flippers to effect a series of slow barrel rolls. It was most certainly sheer fun. She did barrel rolls for minutes at a time, spiraling through the water like a corkscrew. Sometimes she underestimated her speed and started off with too much flipper angle, whipping herself into a snap roll that sent her spinning dizzily out of control. Through repeated trial and error, she learned that a change of head angle was causing her to lose control. She persisted, and by keeping her beak pointed straight ahead, soon learned to execute high speed snap rolls without changing direction or speed.

Next, she perfected a half roll, snapping herself upside down and swimming that way for a while, then righting herself again. She had seen adults do this, using their white underbellies to frighten fish toward the surface.

Within a week, she was flashing through the sea as fast as many adults, and because of her smaller size, making tighter turns than any of them. She was now able to maneuver with mother and friend in the high-speed hunts, and she seldom collided with them. She was no doubt pleased with herself, and sensed that her guardians were pleased, too.

The little dolphin soon learned another vital lesson, again pretty much on her own, and that was the art of pacing herself. She found that she had frequently been wasting energy by sweeping her flukes faster than necessary. For any given speed set by the leaders, there seemed to be an optimum rate of fluke-sweep for her body size. Once she matched the speed of the adults, she often found that she could slow her fluke-sweeps and still keep up with the others.

As she became increasingly aware of these finer points, she began to notice that tickling sensations, which she had long felt but did not understand, seemed to increase or decrease as a function of swimming speed. In the past, her only response to the tickle had been a random twitching of her muscles, but now she noticed that by changing the flex of various muscles ever so slightly, she could eliminate the tickle altogether. When she did, she could feel through sensitive facial nerve endings that her speed increased with no extra effort on her part. Soon her muscles were eliminating the tickle so quickly that she was scarcely conscious of the reaction.

The foregoing is a hypothetical framework for the mechanisms through which dolphins achieve turbulence-free motion through the water. This freedom from turbulence was brought to the attention of scientists when dolphins swimming through bioluminescent water were observed to leave almost no visible wakes.

Mere wisps of light could be seen trailing from the tips of the dolphins' flippers and flukes, whereas seals swimming near the dolphins left highly turbulent wakes. It appears that a dolphin has some sort of laminar flow mechanism that minimizes drag and enables the animal to exceed the theoretical ''hull speed'' limitation for its body ''design.''

The key to this mechanism appears to be variability of body contours. In tests conducted by U.S. Navy scientists during the 1960s, accurate solid wood models of dolphins were immersed in flow tanks. At water flow rates equivalent to moderate swimming speeds, the models exhibited considerable turbulence, thus ruling out the possibility that streamlined body shape alone accounted for the animals' turbulencefree motion. In 1966, Max O. Kramer covered a rigid dolphin model with two thin rubber ''skins'' that had fluid-filled canals sandwiched between them, and demonstrated that such a ''skin'' could reduce the drag of the dolphin model by 40 percent. The U.S. Navy used similar hull coverings to effect dramatic increases in the speed of its submarines. Auguste Piccard proposed that lightly powered submersibles, using sensor-computer-actuator feedback to control skin contours, could cross the Atlantic in thirty-six hours.

In my hypothetical model, the tickling sensations felt by the young dolphin are caused by turbulence, which varies as a function of swimming speed. The dolphin's muscles act to dispel the tickle by effecting slight changes in her body contours, thereby eliminating the turbulence and minimizing drag. After a time, this feedback mechanism becomes essentially automatic.

Of course, an animal's skin would have to be superbly sensitive in order for it to detect small eddies along its body, and the gossamery skin of a dolphin meets this criterion. Dolphins are keenly tactile creatures. They respond exquisitely, often erotically, to gentle caresses. As might be expected, they are also quite sensitive to pain, so much so that their keen sensitivity could hardly serve purely voluptuous purposes. More likely, the nerve endings so richly supplied over their entire body surfaces function as pressure sensors, those in the face sensing swimming speed and/or low-frequency sound waves, while those along the body sense turbulence. Essapian (1955) and Kramer (1960) were among the first to propose such possibilities, and to suggest the existence of active mechanisms for suppression of turbulence.

A related question, posed by one of the scientists who reviewed this book, might best be pondered here. If dolphins are capable of turbulence-free movement, how can their babies ride effortlessly alongside them? How the babies do it may be in question, but they do in fact get a free ride. Several films and videotapes show baby dolphins keeping up with their mothers over considerable distances, without a single flick of their flukes.[2] I examined these scenes closely for signs of physical contact, thinking that the babies might touch their mothers' sides with their flippers, and thus be carried along.[3] There were no discernible prolonged contacts, merely the occasional brushes that might be expected during turning maneuvers.

It is likely that a dolphin baby is swept along by its mother's pressure field. Although turbulence free, or nearly so, a dolphin nonetheless develops a pressure field as the water is displaced by its body and closes in again behind it. Properly positioned in this pressure field, a baby would benefit from such a sustained forward thrust.

As spring passed into summer, the babies became increasingly active and curious. Although usually confined within the boundaries of the herd's formation, they often explored that safe sphere, darting back and forth among the various groups like children cavorting about on a steadily moving train.

In the course of her explorations, the firstborn baby noticed that the swimming positions of certain adults were fairly consistent. The herd was nearly always led by a group comprising two females and one male, all of them quite elderly, judging by their many scars and the paling of their body markings. In time, the baby came to understand that these were the oldest members of the herd. All three had survived for more than twenty years, and the others relied on the accumulated wisdom of their experience to keep the herd well fed and safe from danger.

The baby sensed the difference in these three elders. They seldom played like the other adults, but instead seemed forever preoccupied with finding food and avoiding danger. The first time she approached them, expecting the fond greetings and moments of play the other adults extended to the babies, she found that they merely tolerated—essentially ignored her—as they continued to echo-probe the waters ahead and to taste the signs borne to them on the currents. The feeling of rejection left by that encounter discouraged her from making further approaches.

Far more receptive to her visits were the other groups, most of which comprised females and their offspring of one or more birthings.

The yearling males often played with her and the other babies, and sometimes their play became sexual. Although she as yet had no understanding of sex, she was aware of the differences between the sexes, primarily because the mature males often displayed their penises to the females. As though emulating their elders, the yearling males frequently did the same. In fact, although the yearling males would not become sexually mature until about the age of six, they sometimes went through the motions of trying to copulate with the female babies, but the little ones never remained in one place long enough for the males to succeed.

Eight of the fourteen males in the herd were sexually immature. Three were newborn, and five others were yearlings who still supplemented their fish diets with mothers' milk. The six mature males were well along in years. The herd contained no males or females between the ages of two and six years.

White-sided dolphins between the ages of two and six years are apparently rare in reproductive herds.[4] It is not known whether they voluntarily leave the reproductive herds at about the age of two years, or are driven out, but two recent mass strandings of reproductive herds revealed an absence of animals between the ages of two and six years. On the other hand, there were many animals in this age bracket among the single strandings reported over a recent four-year period. This suggests that immature animals lead solitary lives after leaving the reproductive herds; however, given the highly social nature of dolphins, it seems more likely that juveniles form loose groups. Upon maturation, at about age six, these groups may develop into reproductive herds, but a more plausible scenario would be for maturing individuals to join existing herds led by older, more experienced animals. Without some such means of replenishing losses due to deaths, reproductive herds could no longer sustain themselves, and short herd life would be counterproductive for the species.

In the two stranded reproductive herds, mature females (age six and older) outnumbered mature males by nearly five to one, whereas the immature animals were about evenly divided in terms of sex. These data, together with those previously mentioned, lead to three conclusions: (1) the male and female birth rates are about even, (2) animals of both sexes leave the reproductive herds at about the age of two, and (3) most maturing females (age six or seven) return to reproductive herd life, whereas maturing males tend to remain in bachelor herds. These conclusions are tentative at best, because the data are drawn from only two mass strandings and 30 singly stranded animals, a four-year data base of 121 animals drawn from a population that may well run into the millions.

Why might juvenile animals leave the reproductive herds? It appears not to be a case of older males driving off potential rivals, for it involves both sexes. Maternal rejection is one possible cause. As pregnant females approach term, they undoubtedly force their already weaned youngsters to shift for themselves. Whether the juveniles are allowed to remain or are forcibly ejected may depend on optimum herd size. Many higher mammal species favor social groups of fifty to one hundred individuals and form splinter groups when their numbers exceed optimum levels.

No discussion of cetacean social groups would be complete without some mention of sexual practices, for the popular literature would have us believe that dolphin sexuality is boundless. There are reports of incest, homosexuality, masturbation, interspecific sex, and what seems a general tendency toward sex with any available object or orifice. These reports are perforce based on observations of captive animals, who do find bizarre ways to relieve the boredom of confinement; still, the subject seems blown out of proportion. I have spent countless hours observing captive dolphins of various species, and I find them no more preoccupied with sex than are other captives. Gregory Bateson and Barrie Gilbert observed 7 dolphins at Sea Life Park for 27 days, and recorded only 18 instances of coitus.

If anything, dolphins seem less aggressive about sex than most creatures. Male dolphins seldom fight. Even in captivity, where choice of mates is limited, competition among males usually results in little more than pushing contests. Free dolphins seem to mix quite easily, and it appears that both intraspecific and interspecific copulation occurs between herds.

Why, though, do dolphins seem less aggressive than most animals? Is it because they share sex on a casual basis, or is that an effect rather than a cause? And what of territoriality? Even among nomads whose ranges are vast and whose food supplies are always on the move, might not preferred swimming positions lead to territorial disputes?

Perhaps the major factor minimizing aggression in dolphins is suggested by the herd data presented earlier. Most reproductive herds may be under matriarchal control.

Whatever the reason, dolphins exhibit little aggressive behavior. Dr. Kenneth S. Norris has conducted exhaustive behavioral studies of free dolphins in Hawaiian waters and has seen little fighting among the animals. Nowhere have I found evidence to the contrary.

A calm day, sunny for the most part, though occasional brief showers dimpled the sea. The raindrops plucked faint melodies from the taut surface, and the little female enjoyed the sounds.

The herd came upon an ocean sunfish swimming slowly at a depth of fifty feet, feeding on a swarm of jellyfish. Never had the little female seen such a strange fish. It was eight feet long and just as high, two-thirds of it seeming to consist of head. There was really no tail in the usual sense. The animal looked like a fish whose body had been chopped off just behind the high dorsal and anal fins.[5]

The dolphins stopped and teased the sunfish for a while, pushing it around in circles and nipping the three-foot-high fins. The fish made no attempt to escape. It merely waited until the dolphins had their fun, then continued on, waving its dorsal and anal fins from side to side in a sculling motion and continuously flapping its small pectoral fins to stabilize itself. To change direction, the sunfish squirted strong jets of water from either gill-opening.

As the dolphins moved away, a nine-foot mako closed in and attacked the sunfish. Grasping its quarry by the belly just ahead of the anal fin, the shark whipped its body from side to side, trying to disembowel the sunfish. Failing that, it went for the tail, then tried for a killing bite across the back. Frustrated in its attempts to pierce the seemingly helpless animal's tough hide, the mako circled the sunfish several times, tried one last bite, then moved off in search of less well armored prey.

Once again the sunfish continued on its way, feeding on whatever larvae, plankton, and jellyfish it encountered. Its body showed a few bite marks from the mako's sharp teeth, but no damage had been done. Its leathery skin and three-inch coat of gristle can literally deflect harpoons and bullets. In fact, most ocean sunfish seen in the Gulf of Maine bear scars from boat propellers, yet few seem to die as a result of the collisions.

Ahead now was a large school of menhaden, but before the dolphins could close on them, hundreds of bluefish streaked in from the south and attacked. Killing and maiming far more menhaden than they could possibly eat, the bluefish littered the area with offal. The hissing slaughter moved to the surface. Menhaden leaped from the water in shimmering silver-blue waves, but there was no escaping the snapping jaws. The bluefish whipped the surface into a maelstrom of spray and

61

blood, continuing the carnage long after they had gorged themselves.

Most of the bluefish were little larger than their prey—fifteen to twenty inches long—but menhaden are toothless plankton eaters, while bluefish are piranhas of the sea. Many menhaden were left writhing in their death throes, with single large chunks bitten out of their bodies. Others were hacked to pieces.

The slaughter soon attracted thousands of gulls, who settled on the scene in a screaming white cloud. Some young gulls made the mistake of alighting on the water to claim their share, rather than taking it on the wing. One disappeared in an explosion of feathers and blood. Another flapped back into the air, dangling a bloody stump where its left leg used to be.

The dolphins circled wide around the carnage. The elders knew that bluefish in a feeding frenzy will snap at anything within reach, even whales. Pound for pound, they are among the most feared predators in the sea.[6]

A few miles farther north, the dolphins located a school of herring even larger than the menhaden school decimated by the bluefish. So large was it that the dolphins began separating a manageable number of fish from the main school. Suddenly hundreds of spiny dogfish appeared, killing and maiming the herring with a voracity approaching that of bluefish. The school divided into several subgroups, one of which the dolphins managed to contain, but so numerous and voracious were the dogfish that they disrupted the dolphins' hunt and endangered the babies. The white-sides managed to ram a few of these three-foot sharks, but the rest of the dogfish were in such a feeding frenzy that they scarcely took notice of the dolphins.

The white-sides left the area and continued north. Finding no schools near the surface for a distance of several miles, they began swimming deep, and at a depth of about sixty feet they surprised a school of whiting browsing the banks for sand lances. The dolphins surrounded the whiting and herded them against the "wall" of the surface, where they could more easily be contained. It was a good hunt. Having eaten their fill, they again headed north.

By the following morning, the herd was approaching the northern extremity of Stellwagen Bank. The waters teemed with sand lances, herring, mackerel, and small shrimp. Many whales had gathered to feed, together with several other herds of white-sided dolphins and a group of eleven white-beaked dolphins. Also sharing the finned bounty were four crusty old draggers, on station since sunrise.

A few hours after sunrise, dozens of other vessels appeared from the west, many of them sport fishing boats, whose skippers eagerly awaited the annual return of the bluefin tuna. The great bluefins usually arrive by late May, but the inshore waters were nearly a month late in reaching summer temperatures. During the past week or so, the water had warmed to nearly 60 degrees, and the sport fishermen were out in force.

Seven larger vessels appeared, crowded with passengers who had come to watch the whales. The hailing ports painted on their sterns included Gloucester, Beverly, Portsmouth, and Newburyport.

The whales and dolphins threaded their way among

63

the various vessels, alternating between feeding and watching the people who had come to watch them. A humpback "spy-hopped" close alongside one vessel to look it over, and the passengers screamed with delight.

The dolphins ate their fill of herring, then small groups of them singled out some of the faster-moving finbacks and rode their head waves. It was the first time the little female had played the game, and she was frightened as she followed her mother and nanny into position a few feet ahead of a sixty-foot finback, but her fear was quickly outweighed by the delightful sensation of riding the whale's pressure field. At substantial speed, she coasted along with no effort on her part.

The finback made a sudden turn to the right, and the three dolphins lost the pressure field. Following the whale, they saw the reason for its sharp maneuver. A large school of herring lay ahead.

The finback circled the school, keeping the fish on its right side, where its lower lip, part of its face, and the forward third of its baleen are nearly white. These patches of light coloration on one side of its head serve either to frighten fish or to give the whale's head less definite form thereby confusing its prey. (Scientific opinion is divided on this matter.) As the finback tightened its circle, the herring crowded together. The whale then turned and lunged at the school, scooping tons of water and fish into its gaping mouth, expanding its pleated throat and forebelly until it appeared to have a titanic case of mumps. Now the whale closed its mouth, constricted the muscles around its pleats to force the water out through its baleen, and swallowed a hundred or more herring.

It was an amazing sight. The entire herd of dolphins might take an hour to catch the number of fish the whale swallowed with a single gulp!

When the finback slowed to rest, the dolphins, seeking more active playmates, overtook a passing minke. This twenty-five-foot whale seemed to share their spirit of play and, accelerating to twenty knots, even porpoising a few times, it cleared the water like a dolphin. The dolphins flanked the minke and leaped in unison with it, to excited cries from a nearby vessel.

When they tired of playing with the minke, the dolphins cast about the area, whistle-calling in search of their comrades. Hearing familiar whistle replies, they headed toward the sounds; then suddenly the two adults popped to the surface and looked south. The baby surfaced between them and saw a large flock of herring gulls and black-back gulls skimming the water in her direction, as though following a whale in the hope of sharing its catch. Moments later, fish of many different species flashed past the dolphins, heading north. Behind the horde of fish appeared a sweeping arc of bluefin tuna, fifteen or twenty in all, maintaining such precise intervals from each other that they formed a nearly perfect parabola, its concave side facing forward. As fish were forced into the focal point of their formation, the bluefins closed ranks and caught what they could, then regrouped and continued their parabolic sweep.

The bluefin tuna in this hunting school are about four feet long. Each fish would tip the scales at approximately four hundred pounds. Handsomely streamlined, they have dark blue backs, white bellies, and white flanks with silvery spots. Their colors fade to a uniform dull gray soon after death, so anglers landing bluefins have little time to appreciate their beauty.

As the young dolphin and the two adults rejoined the herd, they saw several more schools of bluefins, each containing tuna of about the same size. The smaller the tuna, the larger the schools seemed to be. The dolphins also encountered solitary adult bluefins measuring eight or nine feet in length and weighing eight hundred to a thousand pounds. The little dolphin could not contend with the speed of these adult bluefins. Some of them flashed past her at forty to fifty knots. The largest bluefins seem to hunt alone for the most part, probably because they are so fast that they have less need of cooperative hunts.

Boat radios crackled the news that the first bluefins had been sighted, and the area soon swarmed with sport fishing vessels.

The whales and dolphins moved north to quieter, less crowded waters, and the whale-watching vessels followed them. Over the southern reaches of Jeffreys Ledge, the whales began emitting low-frequency echolocation sounds, and soon detected vast swarms of sand lances (known to local fishermen as sand eels because of their eel-like fins and swimming movements). The slender little ammodytes, four to six inches long at maturity, are highly prized by large whales, in part because of the vast numbers in which they school.

A great hunt was begun by the various cetaceans, whose numbers now included nine humpback whales, four finbacks, two minkes, and three herds of white-sided dolphins.

Finback and minke whales rely largely on speed to catch their food, but the slower humpbacks have some altogether different and dramatically effective ways of hunting.

As soon as they detect small prey such as sand lances, humpbacks begin diving under the schools and releasing enormous clouds of bubbles from their blow-holes. Each bubble-cloud drives hundreds, even thousands of sand lances toward the surface. The whales follow their bubble-clouds to the surface and thrust their heads out of the water with mouths agape, catching large numbers of sand lances with each gulp.

Gulls are well aware of humpback hunting methods and are quick to take advantage of them. As each bubble-cloud reaches the surface, forming a lime green flat spot about twenty feet in diameter, gulls converge on it from all directions. Some gulls are able to anticipate the clouds from a hundred yards away, long before the bubbles show, perhaps because they hear the bubbles rising or see them well below the surface.

Each surfacing humpback is mobbed by screaming gulls, who snatch food out of the water cascading over the whale's lips. Some gulls even hover inside the whales' open mouths to get their share of the catch. So many gulls mob surface-feeding humpbacks that observers aboard nearby vessels are often lucky if they can see, let alone photograph, the whales.

Sometimes three or more humpbacks blow bubble-clouds so close together that they appear to be using co-operative feeding methods to contain prey within the confines of multiple bubble-clouds. Each whale usually surfaces inside its own bubble-cloud, though, so it is more likely that several whales are simply trapping various portions of one large school.

Humpbacks do not always use bubble-clouds. If they happen upon prey that is already at the surface, the whales simply lunge-feed, breaking the surface with their mouths open and swallowing their catch on the move. Sometimes they lunge-feed through the tops of bubble-clouds, rather than surfacing heads up inside them. In some instances, such behavior smacks of pilferage, for certain whales appear to reap the benefits of bubble-clouds blown by other whales. In such cases, a second whale usually surfaces so close beside the first that they are almost touching. If indeed some whales are filching the fruits of others' labors, there are no signs of violent objections or retaliation. The apparent thieves may be juveniles being assisted by their mothers until they master the skills of bubble-cloud feeding.

The gulls have their best opportunities when the humpbacks surface heads up inside their bubble-clouds. Lunging above the surface with its mouth wide open, each whale traps tons of water and fish inside its pleated throat pouch. The throat becomes so grotesquely distended with water that it ripples and heaves in the swells like a massive water-filled balloon. So great is the volume of water contained in the humpback's mouth and throat pouch that it takes the whale a few moments to close its jaws, and the gulls put these moments to good use. Plunging quickly in and out of the whale's mouth, or swimming close and reaching in with their heads, the birds gobble up as many fish as they can before the great jaws close and the whale constricts the muscles around its pleats to force out the water, trapping the catch in its fringed baleen plates.

Bubble-cloud feeding is a common summer sight in the Gulf of Maine. Humpbacks are also seen using bubble-nets, which are marked by the gradual formation of bubble-rings on the surface as whales circle below, releasing cylindrical air curtains around their prey. The whales surface inside the completed bubble-nets, usually thrusting their heads well out of the water as they swallow.

When and why do humpbacks favor one bubble formation over the other? Here are some possible answers.

A bubble-net concentrates prey inside a cylinder, through which the whale rises like a piston, compressing its food into a dense mass at the surface. Bubble-clouds (quicker and easier to form) may be used on prey that is already concentrated, simply driving it to the surface.

The choice of bubble-cloud versus bubble-net may also be dictated by the size of prey. Small creatures may be forced bodily to the surface by bubble-clouds. Larger prey would be frightened by, and contained within, bubble-nets.

Finally, skill could be a deciding factor. It may take many years for a humpback to master the art of bubble-net feeding. Those humpback whales seen using this technique may for the most part be the older, more experienced animals.

When humpbacks surface-feed in coastal fisheries, hovering gulls gather, stealing fish and beclouding the photographs of whale watchers. Experienced photographers turn this to their advantage by focusing their cameras on an area toward which the gulls are converging. A whale usually appears in their viewfinders. The trick is to photograph the whale before it becomes festooned with gulls.

This game of stealing fish from whales is not without its perils, for the remains of gulls and other seabirds have been found in the stomachs of humpbacks. The birds may have tried to filch one fish too many as the whales were closing their mouths, or may have been caught napping on the surface during lunge-feeding maneuvers. The whales probably had no intention of eating the birds, but who can say for certain? Mobbed by screaming, pecking gulls whenever they surface-feed over coastal fishing banks, humpbacks may delight in swallowing a few of the noisy nuisances.

The intense feeding activity continued for an hour or more, then the humpbacks settled down to rest. Moving very slowly, sometimes floating motionless with their backs awash for minutes at a time, they napped and digested their meal. The skippers of the whale-watching vessels maintained respectful distances from the resting whales, but several small power boats maneuvered too close. The humpbacks sharply arched their backs, and with graceful fluke displays, went deep.

The finbacks and minkes had long ago gone their separate ways. Only the dolphins remained, mopping up the remaining sand lances and a few schools of short-finned squid that had been feeding on the lances.

The whale-watching vessels set off in search of other whales, and the small yachts went their various ways.

Soon the dolphins headed northeasterly along Jeffreys Ledge. Many herring gulls and black-back gulls followed, perhaps hoping the dolphins would lead them to the great whales, which were swimming too deep and staying down too long to be tracked from the air. When the coastline began slipping below the horizon, most of the gulls turned back, tacking across a brisk southwesterly breeze toward shore.

Four

AS THE DOLPHINS HEADED NORTHEASTERLY along Jeffreys Ledge, the naturalists' marine radios were buzzing with the news that a pod of orcas had been sighted near the Isles of Shoals. A whale-watching vessel out of Gloucester reported that the orcas were swimming close to the rocks on Duck Island, possibly hoping to pick off newly weaned pups from the islands' harbor seal colony. Followed by the vessel, the pod of seven orcas headed easterly toward Jeffreys Ledge.

That night, as the three white-side herds rested and socialized following an evening hunt, the firstborn female heard strange sounds from the west. Pitched midway between the birdlike chirps of dolphins and the sonorous voices of great whales, the trumpeting calls continued for several minutes, subtle differences in timbre suggesting that several animals were making the sounds. The young female also heard faint clicks similar

72

to those made by white-sided dolphins, but heavier and more powerful, reminiscent of the echo-clicks made by sperm whales.

Recognizing the sounds of orcas, most feared of all predators in the sea, the white-side elders became agitated. The two groups that had spent the past twelve hours with the firstborn female's herd suddenly moved off toward the south and east. The various groups in the young female's herd moved this way and that, vocalizing at length, as though trying to decide which direction to take. Finally, the herd resumed its northeasterly journey over Jefferys Ledge. Orca cries were heard again from time to time, but they sounded no closer than before. The little female wished the sounds would stop, for each time the distant calls were heard, the heartbeats of her mother and nanny accelerated.

Midmorning found the dolphins over the eastern periphery of Jeffreys Ledge, where they came upon a sight that made even the most seasoned elders rear back at the surface to look. Cold upwellings from the six hundred-foot depths beyond the ledge had condensed the warm, moist air into a thick cloud of fog one hundred feet high. Like the sheer face of a glacier, the fog bank extended for miles along Jeffreys Ledge, looming stark white against deep blue sea and sky.

Following the edge of the fog bank, the dolphins played now-you-see-me, now-you-don't by darting in and out of the thick mist. Ahead, a dragger completed a trawl along the ledge, turned east into deeper water to retrieve its net, and dissolved into whiteness. Its foghorn moaned, and was answered by other horns within and beyond the fog bank.

Over Jeffreys Ledge, the calm surface quivered with life as the dolphins fed at their leisure on menhaden, sand lances, herring, mackerel, and squid. So thick were the schools that the dolphins were able to catch their fill without using echolocation. The silence was apparently purposeful, for any sucklings breaking it were admonished.

About midday, orca calls were heard again, much closer now, and spread over a fairly wide arc to the south. Minutes later, a school of several hundred bluefin tuna, all about two years of age and weighing twenty pounds or less, passed near the dolphins, heading north. The young tuna were not spread out as they would be when hunting, but were tightly massed, and moved with the single-minded restless precision of obligatory schoolers stalked by predators.

The dolphin elders faced south and listened for telltale underwater sounds, then reared back with their heads above water to scan the surface. Several miles south, at the edge of the fog, six gannets burst into the air as though frightened. The dolphins headed quietly toward the fog bank a mile to the east, probably seeking deeper water, which would offer more maneuvering room and perhaps some scattering layers to screen them from the orcas' sonar.

More orca cries, closer still, came from the south. A school of four-year-old fifty-pound bluefins passed under the dolphins, heading north, tightly massed like the others. The dolphins accelerated to twenty knots, but instead of porpoising to save energy, they swam well below the surface and broke water very quietly each time they breathed. They were fifty yards from the fog bank, when an eight-foot bluefin tuna flashed below and ahead of them at forty knots, totally ignoring the schools of fish bursting all around it. Moments later, the dolphins heard the thud of heavy bodies colliding.

A twenty-five-foot orca materialized from the mist, rearing out of the water to his flippers, his jaws clamped around the giant bluefin's head. The eight-hundred-pound bluefin struggled mightily, but its movements merely helped the orca to effect a crippling bite through the gills. The orca's snowy throat and chest ran red with blood, then with a dull snap, the tuna's spine broke and the great fish went limp. Still holding the bluefin by the head, the whale sank back into the water. A sixteen-foot female surfaced beside him and severed the tuna's tail to ensure that it could not escape.

Another female orca appeared, and leaving the dying bluefin to sink, the three whales spread out to lie in wait. Other orca screams were heard from the south, then the water near the edge of the fog began roiling like a tidal rip. The three orcas inhaled and quietly submerged as many large bluefins and myriad other assorted fish approached their area, urged on by the cries of the whales behind them.

The dolphins slipped quietly back the way they had come.

The fish blundered into the three waiting orcas, who launched a slashing attack, swallowing smaller fish as they went, crippling larger tuna by severing their caudal fins. All the while, their chilling cries threw the fish into an even greater panic. Some tuna escaped below or to

75

either side, but many circled in confusion long enough for the other orcas to sweep in from the south and close the trap.

Realizing they were surrounded, some older and wiser bluefins tried to go deep, but two orcas had anticipated that, and were already diving below them. The surface exploded as several large tuna sought safety in the air, only to ensure their deaths by falling back into waiting jaws. Concentrating on the largest bluefins, the whales worked in pairs, one orca sweeping in from the front to distract and slow the tuna while the other bit off its tail. Each bluefin thus injured was left thrashing helplessly, while its attackers darted off to cripple another fish. Within minutes, the orcas disabled twenty or more tuna weighing from two hundred to six hundred pounds.

Including the huge fish crippled earlier, the orcas' kill totaled more than three tons. Enormous though this figure may seem, it is less than the day's requirement for these highly active mammals whose metabolism demands a daily food intake exceeding 10 percent of body weight. This extended family of seven whales, ranging in size from a three-ton juvenile to a nine-ton male, required about four tons of food each day.

Concentrating first on the fish that had not yet sunk to the bottom, the orcas bit off ham-size portions and swallowed them whole. When they had consumed all the sinking fish, the whales dove deep and echolocated the rest of the tuna, still struggling on the bottom. As feeding continued at a leisurely pace for thirty minutes or more, a spreading stain of blood and oil was carried afar by the currents, attracting thousands of dogfish and other sharks.

When they had eaten the last of the bluefins, the orcas gathered at the surface and dozed with their backs awash while the sharks and other fishes cleaned up the offal from their kill. Borne on a gentle current, the napping orcas slowly disappeared into the fog bank.

By the time the orcas began feeding, the dolphins were well on their way south toward Stellwagen Bank. They may well have nothing to fear from the orcas, as long as the bluefin tuna—the orcas' major reason for being in the area—remain in abundance. With only seven orcas hunting over a large area, the chances are good that they will not disrupt the bluefin population. On the other hand, if these seven are merely part of a larger orca pod, the bluefins may abandon their favorite summer fishing banks en masse. Should that happen, the orcas will resort to any available prey, which could include dolphins and even great whales. The whitesides will keep as much distance as possible between the orcas and themselves.

The relationship of dolphins to their larger cousins, the orcas, is not always a clear-cut one of prey versus predator. It is common knowledge that captive orcas swim peaceably with dolphins, apparently because a steady source of food suppresses the orcas' predatory instincts. Less well known, and quite surprising, is the fact that peaceful coexistence is also possible in the wild. Dolphins have been photographed swimming close to orcas in the sea.[1] In June 1982, a lone orca was reportedly seen close to the Isles of Shoals, swimming companionably with several Atlantic white-sided dolphins.

Prey animals can sense when predators are not hunting, and will allow such predators to pass quite close. Still, for dolphins to swim alongside orcas seems tantamount to wildebeests frolicking in the midst of a lion pride. Perhaps dolphins do this only when they feel that they can outmaneuver the orcas. The aforementioned cases did involve single orcas with groups of dolphins; however, in 1978 Richard Elliot observed a single white-sided dolphin swimming with two orcas.[2]

Food abundance or preference may determine orca behavior toward dolphins. Some pods of orcas in the Pacific Northwest eat fish exclusively, while others include marine mammals in their diets. As for the dolphins' behavior, perhaps they simply echo-sense when an orca's stomach is full, and act accordingly. A well-fed orca may be a safe orca. Then again, well-fed orcas may be playful, and their idea of play can be macabre. Observers in Patagonia tell of orcas repeatedly lobbing sea lions thirty feet in the air with their flukes, as though playing a game.[3] Orcas are also known to flip seals and sea lions about with their heads, toying with them like a cat with a mouse. Stomach conditions notwithstanding, such animals would appear to be risky swim companions.

Maybe dolphins are attracted to orcas for the same reasons they seem drawn to people—a fascination with power, perhaps? After all, we and the orcas rule the seas, and dolphins may be sufficiently intrigued by *Orcinus orca* and *Homo sapiens* to take certain calculated risks.

Swimming over Stellwagen Bank about fifteen miles off Cape Ann, the white-sides noticed to the east of them, where only open ocean should be, a dense cluster of masts such as they normally saw only when passing near harbors. Moving closer, they found a large gathering of lofty sport fishing vessels.

Anchored against wind and currents, and accompanied by a two hundred-foot "buy boat," the anglers were still-fishing with large bait mackerel for the great tuna that frequent this area every summer and make it one of the world's richest giant bluefin fisheries.

Until the advent in the 1970s of the Japanese market for large bluefins, this type of fishing was done strictly for sport. Banned for human consumption in the United States and Canada because of high mercury levels in the flesh, the noble fish sold for about twenty cents a pound in 1970, and were ground up for pet food. From 1971 on, Japanese market demands drove prices steadily upward, and as of 1984 fishermen were being paid $2.50 per pound for tuna "on the hoof." What used to be sport has become highly lucrative business, so the reports of orcas hunting the banks have the tuna fishermen concerned. Each large bluefish eaten by orcas represents $2,000 or more out of some fisherman's pocket, so the stage is set for a clash between killer whales and fishermen.

The dolphins passed well below the tuna boats, weaving their way among the anchor lines and fishing lines that slanted out of sight into the shadowy depths. Distracted momentarily by loud rock music transmitted through the hull of one boat, a juvenile male snagged his right flipper on a fishing line. On the boat above, a reel whined briefly, bringing the man in the fighting chair bolt upright, gripping his rod in eager anticipation. The young male disengaged himself from the line and caught up with the others, while the fisherman reeled in to check his bait.

As the dolphins surfaced far beyond the tuna boats, they heard heavy blows being struck against the water, and turned westerly to investigate. A mile or more toward shore, they saw several vessels and, rising from their midst, the tall white flipper of a humpback whale. As they watched, the flipper swung down against the surface with a whump that was audible for miles, then rose and struck the water again and again.

Moving closer, the dolphins found two humpback whales lazing about at the surface, surrounded by boats crowded with whale watchers. One of the whales was floating on his side, raising his right flipper and striking it against the water. The other whale floated quietly nearby with her head and back awash, apparently dozing until one of the male's flipper-slaps grazed her flank, at which point she gently swung her flukes against him and pushed herself away to continue her nap at a safe distance.

Propelled by the female's fluke thrust, the male drifted belly up alongside one of the boats. Excited passengers leaned over the rail, only to be greeted by a leviathan fart that sent several persons tumbling backwards. Men laughed. Women blushed. Children asked parents embarrassing questions. The whale rolled onto his side and released a great gush of rust-colored feces, then slipped quietly below the surface to check out the clicking sounds coming from the other side of the boat.

Unnoticed by the whale watchers, the white-sides had been diving deep a few hundred yards from the boats to hunt silver hake, which had gathered in considerable numbers to prey on sand lances. Intent on catching the speedy young hakes, the dolphins failed to notice the humpback as he dove far below them. The first sign of his presence was a great cloud of bubbles that suddenly rose toward them.

The firstborn female's nanny was away from her side at the time, busy catching her share of fish. This had left the young dolphin on the outside of the herd's formation. She was swimming only a body length or two away from her mother, but when the bubble-cloud engulfed them, she became separated from the group. Visually and acoustically confused by the loudly fizzing mass, she darted this way and that in search of clear water, only to find herself popping to the surface, surrounded by screaming gulls and leaping sand lances.

Bubble-cloud . . . sand lances . . . gulls. Her memory filled in the rest of the picture, and she leaped away from the patch of effervescent green water. As she did so, her flukes struck something that felt like an enormous rock. Just then the humpback surfaced, his gaping mouth engulfing the patch of water which a moment before had contained herself.

As the whale surged past her, skimming his lower jaw along the surface, she saw his great brown eye roll back to look at her. He showed the white of his eye, as though surprised to see her there, then dipped his right flipper safely clear below the young dolphin and turned toward her. The little female was about to dart away, when her mother and nanny surfaced beside her. Emboldened by their presence, she held her position as the whale glided slowly by. When his eye was directly opposite her, he swept his flippers forward and stopped about fifteen feet away, then brought his right flipper within a foot of her.[4] Very brave now, she touched her beak to the knobby flipper and made a squealing blowhole sound. The whale responded with a trumpet blow that sent her darting behind her guardians.

Now the whale lowered his right flipper and used his left to scull himself closer to the dolphins. When his head was a few feet away, he rolled until his eye was at surface level and studied them for several minutes, first from below the surface and then from above. Ever so slowly, he raised his flipper until it was gently brushing their undersides. The little dolphin's fear of the great beast drained suddenly away, and she began swimming all around him. The whale submerged and moved ahead, doing slow barrel rolls just below the surface while the young female swam loops around him. Now he swam on his back with the tips of his flippers cutting the surface, while she darted back and forth between them.

Soon the entire white-side herd joined in the fun, riding the whale's head wave, doing figure eights around his flippers, and swimming close alongside to peer into his great brown eyes. Their play carried them far from the other humpback, who still lay napping at the surface, surrounded by vessels.

A sixty-foot fishing boat approached from the north about a quarter-mile away, moving parallel to the whale's heading. Apparently fishing was not the vessel's purpose this day, for its afterdeck was crowded with sightseers. The humpback spy-hopped and looked the boat over, then headed directly toward it. The skipper shut down his engines, and the vessel glided quietly to a stop.[5] Curious as to what the whale was up to, the dolphins followed him.

As though meeting an old friend, the humpback sidled right up to the sixty-foot boat, then dove under the bow and proceeded to rub his back against the soft marine growth hanging from the hull. Using his flippers to thrust himself back and forth, he drifted the full length of the vessel, rubbing his back against the mossy marine growth.

Surfacing at the stern, he blew his fishy breath into the beaming faces of a dozen whale watchers, some of whom nearly fell over the side in their attempts to touch him. The whale rolled until his right eye cleared the water, and with his flipper poised high in the air, regarded the people with a gaze that was incapable of expression, yet somehow left little doubt as to the gentleness of his intentions. It was as though he too craved contact, and the people lining the rail were beside themselves with the emotion of the moment.

Even the skipper and his crew, hard-bitten fishermen one might expect to wrench a living from the sea with little regard for its inhabitants, leaned over the rail and shared their passengers' excitement. The naturalist guiding the expedition stood on the cabin top, his camera hanging forgotten around his neck as he savored the magic of the moment. He told the people that they called this whale Puck, because of the mark shaped like a hockey stick on the underside of his flukes. Puck, he said, was one of many humpbacks in the area who seem openly affectionate toward people on boats. Having said that, he watched in rapt silence.

There was no need for the naturalist to say anything more. In his way, the whale was speaking more eloquently for the preservation of his kind than any advocate could hope to do. For most of the sightseers aboard that boat, the slogan "Save the Whales" had already taken on new and deeply personal meaning.

Time for another back rub. Slowly, the whale rolled upright and thrust himself ahead with a leisurely sweep of his flukes. Several persons standing at the stern backed away as they saw the fifteen-foot flipper descending toward them, but the humpback folded the flipper flat against his side before completing the roll, then moved slowly toward the bow, all the while looking up at the people leaning over the port rail.

When he reached the bow, the whale again dove athwartships and, using his flippers to thrust himself back and forth, gently rubbed himself against the hull as a slight current carried him aft. Each time he surfaced at the stern, he paused to roll and look up at the people before returning to the bow.

For nearly an hour, the whale repeated this routine, then at last he sounded and swam away.

Few can help but be moved when a forty to fifty ton whale, easily capable of crushing their vessel and killing everyone aboard, sidles up alongside like a curious, gentle pup. To stand in the presence of such awesome power, and feel safe in the doing, evokes a strong sense of gratitude and kinship. It is tantamount to having a wild elephant approach and gently investigate you with its trunk.

What large wild animals other than cetaceans will even tolerate, let alone initiate, such intimate contact? Few, if any. Some park animals will approach people for handouts, but that is hardly the same as being befriended by whales and dolphins who need nothing from us save the freedom to conduct normal lives. Considering how ruthlessly we have slaughtered these animals, we are not deserving of their trust. Still, they reach out to us in a childlike way, and that is a sacred sort of trust that should never be violated.

Some good people struggling to save cetaceans base their advocacy on the possibility that the animals rank second only to ourselves in terms of intelligence. That may be, but even if proven, it would matter little to the small minority who profit from the slaughter. As for the rest of us, we seem apathetic about the widespread annual slaughter of our own kind, so how can we be expected to rally en masse against the slaughter of whales, however bright they may be? Never mind for now where cetaceans may rank in some arbitrary periodic table of creature worth. They have the power to kill us, yet they trust us and are gentle toward us; reasons enough to let them live.

The only way to stop the killing is to make it

unprofitable. As of 1984, the major whaling nations are Japan and the Soviet Union; together, they account for about 80 percent of the kills.[6] Perhaps only our government can bring pressure to bear upon the Soviet Union, but each of us can have an impact on the Japanese by boycotting their products and making known our reasons. This is not easy. Many Japanese imports are excellent values, and boycotting them involves some sacrifice. If you feel disinclined to make such sacrifices, go out to sea and watch the whales. If you are fortunate, you will experience something along the lines of the preceding scene. Then perhaps, you will find yourself boycotting the goods of whaling nations and writing the manufacturers to explain why you are doing so.[7]

The ultimate victory and irony will come when former whaling vessels are converted for whale-watching cruises and cetological research. That time may not be far off. Already, whale watching may well be grossing more money worldwide than whale killing.

While the humpback rubbed its back against the boat, the dolphins rested a short distance away, swimming slowly at the surface. The firstborn dolphin found herself frequently looking toward the vessel. Sometimes she made the squealing blowhole sound to which the whale had responded earlier, as if calling it to return and play with her, but there was no reply. She felt drawn to the whale, but the white-side herd preferred to maintain a safe distance from vessels.

Hunger growled. She nudged her mother's mammary slits and received spurts of thick milk. After only three swallows, she abandoned the slit. She was tiring of milk, beginning to long for other food, but without teeth she could not catch fish and hold them long enough to swallow. Soon, though, she would have teeth like the adults. Already, her gums were beginning to ache. A strand of kelp floated nearby. She swam over, dragged it back to the sleep circle, and chewed on it while she napped. The rubbery plant eased the dull ache in her gums.

The sound of screaming gulls brought her fully awake. She slipped out of the sleep circle and reared back at the surface to locate the source of the sound. A few hundred yards away, gulls were mobbing a surfacing humpback. Could it be her friend? The whale skimmed the surface for a considerable distance, then dove in her direction. She wanted to swim toward it, but dared not venture that far from her mother.

A few minutes later, she heard air being released far below. Gulls raced toward her as a bubble-cloud appeared out of the depths, expanding as it rose, now forming a fizzing green circle on the surface within a hundred feet of her. A whale lunged through the top of the bubble-cloud with mouth agape, then swam with its lower jaw planing the surface while water squirted from the corners of its mouth. Dozens of gulls fed on the leavings. One herring gull alighted on the humpback's snout and enjoyed a fifty-yard ride before the whale sounded.

This must be her friend. He was the only whale she had seen skim the surface for so long after making a catch. She swam a few yards from the sleep circle, returned, ventured a bit farther away, then returned again, all the while making the squealing sound to which her friend had responded earlier. The humpback whale surfaced almost a quarter-mile away, heading in the opposite direction.

Sadly disappointed, the young dolphin was turning to rejoin the sleep circle when she saw gulls pursuing a mound of water that was moving directly toward her. He had heard her! He was returning!

It appeared that the whale would pass so close that she need swim only a short distance from the sleep circle to intercept him. She swung away from her mother's side and headed toward the mound, which suddenly disappeared. Too late, she realized that this was no humpback whale. Before she could turn and dash back to safety, she was tumbled beak over flukes as a seventy-foot finback whale swept past her in a ten-knot turn. The mound she had seen was caused by the whale skimming the surface with its mouth open. Now it had closed its mouth and was turning away just below the surface to make another skimming run through a swarm of krill that had appeared. Fortunately, as the whale turned its flukes caused such a surge of water that she was hurled clear and narrowly avoided being struck by the great tail.

The surge from the whale's turning maneuver caused the circling dolphins to bump into each other, and the sleep circle was disbanded. Still frightened by her close brush with the swift finback, the young female meekly resumed her place between mother and nanny as the dolphins milled about, listening and tasting the signs borne to them on the currents. With time, the young dolphin would learn to recognize the various species of whales at a distance, and would come to understand that finbacks tend to be less gregarious and playful than humpbacks. Already, she had a keen appreciation of their speed—twenty knots is nothing out of the ordinary for finbacks—and would be more cautious in the future.

A whale-watching vessel passed within a few hundred yards of the milling dolphins, making high-speed maneuvers as the captain attempted to give his passengers a closer look at the feeding finback. After ten minutes of futile pursuit, the expedition's naturalist announced over the loudspeakers that they had been given the "finback slip."

My first close encounter with large whales occurred in August of 1971, ten miles east of Gloucester, Massachusetts. We were cruising at low speed, taking the morning sun on the flying bridge and enjoying a fine, calm day. I happened to be looking off to port, watching a sailboat, when my friend Beverly shouted, "My God, a whale!" Her shout was punctuated by what sounded like an old locomotive releasing a blast of steam close off our starboard bow, but by the time I rose to look, the whale had sounded. Beverly said the whale had gone under the boat, so I idled the engines and shifted into neutral.

Moments later, I heard another blast of air behind me, and spun around (heart in mouth, I might add) to see a finback easily twice the length of my 33-foot boat surfacing close aboard on the port quarter. Aside from a near collision with a sperm whale while I was serving in

89

submarines, I had never before been that close to a large whale, and I had no idea what to expect. As I stood there, gauging the size of the animal, my boat seemed to become progressively smaller.

We soon heard more blows all around us and discovered that we were in the midst of at least a dozen whales. (A later count revealed the total to be fifteen.) The group included two mother-calf pairs. The calves were about twenty feet long, which was a good deal longer than my boat appeared to me by then. I decided to test my radio, in case it became necessary to broadcast a Mayday call.

My fascination must have outweighed my fear, because I soon found myself shutting down the engines so that we could hear the whales' blows more clearly. That may have encouraged the whales to remain nearby. At any rate, those finbacks proceeded to circle us for the next seven and one-half hours, often passing within thirty feet of the boat. Even the mothers and calves came quite close at times. From the flying bridge, we had an outstanding view of them.

During all that time the whales remained near us, I saw no signs of surface feeding, though they could have been diving deep to feed. (The depth-sounder readings averaged about 180 feet in the area over which we drifted that day.) The finbacks seemed to spend most of the time at the surface, usually circling us at leisurely speeds. Perhaps they were resting.

The only exuberant activity occurred when one whale breached about fifty yards from the boat, clearing the water with all but its flukes, then leaning back and to one side as it thundered into the sea. The waves caused by its re-entry set my boat rocking violently. The whale opened its mouth as it leaped, enabling us to see the baleen hanging from the upper jaw. We also got a clear view of the longitudinal pleats in the throat and forebelly. I recall seeing a large reddish orange patch near the flipper. There are no records of such coloration in finbacks, so the patch may have been an abrasion. Perhaps the whale had scraped its body against the bottom while feeding, the patch also could have been caused by a shark bite.

After the whales had been with us for a few hours, Beverly broke out one of the rods and baited up to do a bit of bottom-fishing. It never occurred to us that this might not be a wise thing to do with the whales nearby.

As Beverly sat at the taffrail and lowered the weighted hook to the bottom, we noticed one whale, which had been circling us about fifty yards out, make a sharp turn toward us from dead astern, and sound. Not daring to reel in at that point, we gripped the rail and waited, voicing fervent hopes that the whale had nothing violent in mind. Suddenly the fishing line, which had been extending straight down into the water, swung out at a 45 degree angle to starboard, bounced several times as it dragged along the whale's side, then swung back to the vertical. Moments later, the whale surfaced about fifty yards ahead of the boat, and resumed its circling.

Thank God the whale passed safely clear of the hook. Had the animal snagged itself, the scene might not have remained so peaceful. Judging by the angle the fishing line assumed, though, the whale was probably not very deep when it rubbed against it. Beverly decided to play it safe, and did no more fishing that day.

From among all the many and varied sounds that whale must have been hearing through the surrounding waters, it immediately sensed the introduction of our fishing line into its environment. How it did so is a mystery. The reel was well oiled, spinning freely, making little noise. The sinker was well above the hook; there should have been no clink of metal against metal. How could the whale hear the line descending? It is possible that the finback saw Beverly lowering the line, but I was watching the whale at the time, and its eyes were nowhere near the surface. I doubt that it could have seen the line through the water from fifty or more yards away, especially in water that was probably turbid with plankton. The whale must have heard something. Perhaps the line made a slight strumming sound as the sinker held it taut in a tidal current. Whatever sense the whale used, the incident demonstrated how keenly aware these animals are.

That day was a rare experience, even more so than I realized at the time, for finbacks seldom tolerate boats among them for minutes, let alone hours. By the time the whales finally left us late that afternoon, my perspective on life in the sea had forever changed. I soon began studying cetaceans at every opportunity, and have continued to do so ever since. I shall probably do so for the rest of my life.

Five

It was a clear, gentle August morning. Small, scattered patches of cloud drifted high overhead, like sheep shearings blown across a blue meadow. A light southwesterly breeze was bunching the ocean's surface into small conical waves. The tide was slack, and surface activity was light.

An hour after sunrise, the tide turned. Deep currents struck the faces of the banks and were deflected toward the surface, sweeping with them diatoms, copepods, euphausians, and other planktonic life forms. The combined effect of the cold upwellings and the plankton they carried with them flattened the surface like a great oil slick on the deeper side of each bank. Soon tidal lines extended for miles across the surface, sharply defined boundaries marked by wind-riffled water on the shallower sides and flat, calm water over the depths.

As soon as the tidal lines formed, surface activity increased, especially in the areas of flat water near the lines. The small euphausiid shrimp commonly known as krill were particularly abundant this morning, coloring large patches of sea brick red as they swarmed by the millions near the surface, feeding on phytoplankton. These small crustaceans are highly prized by many species of fish and by all baleen whales. Within an hour of the tide's turning, myriad forms of life were churning the surface along the tidal boundaries.

The white-sides concentrated their first hunt of the morning on a large school of short-finned squid, but they later sampled other fare, even ingesting occasional mouthfuls of krill. Now in their fifth month, the sucklings were beginning to investigate various supplements to their milk diets. Curious by nature and inclined to follow their mothers' examples, many of them had been trying unsuccessfully to catch fish. Now, as the mothers led them through the dense swarms of krill, the youngsters got their first taste of shrimp.

The firstborn female found it fairly easy to plunge into a cloud of krill and come out with at least a small mouthful. The crunchy shrimp were a tasty departure from her mother's milk. Two of the youngest babies were apparently not quite ready for solid food, though. Soon after they ate the krill, they retched them up again.

Many great whales were feeding over this same area of Jeffreys Ledge. Within visual range of the dolphins were thirteen humpbacks, six finbacks, and two minkes. The young female noticed that few humpbacks were using bubble-clouds to catch the krill; most were simply lunge-feeding at the surface. Some worked in pairs, one whale lunge-feeding on its side while the other swam belly down and slightly ahead, deflecting the krill into its partner's open mouth. When one whale had gathered a mouthful and swallowed, the whales reversed roles. Sometimes three whales fed cooperatively, the two on the outside deflecting krill into the open mouth of the whale in the middle.[1]

As usual, the feeding humpbacks attracted many herring gulls and black-back gulls, but also present today were dozens of greater shearwaters, who mixed in quite boldly among the gulls to get their share of krill and small fishes. Now and then an aggressive black-back spread its five-foot wings and loudly challenged the shearwaters' right to be there, but for the most part the gulls were too busy feeding to waste time in territorial disputes.

Wilson's storm petrels—petite dark cousins to the greater shearwaters—skimmed the surface in the wake of each feeding whale, darting this way and that as they snatched up small organisms brought to the surface by the whale's passage. As they pattered along the surface to avoid being dunked by waves, the little tubenoses seemed to walk on water, their white rump patches like snowflakes dancing on the sea.

This habit of pattering along the surface led early sailors to dub petrels "Jesus birds." The word "petrel" is thought to stem from the name Peter (specifically Saint Peter), and to be rooted in this seeming ability to walk on water.

The order of birds known as shearwaters are named for their unique ability to skim (shear) the surface, closely following the contours of waves for long distances without beating their wings. One greater shearwater was seen to glide for 1.5 miles without a single wing-beat. It appears that they do this by riding the boundary layer of denser air just above the ocean's surface. This is conjecture on my part, but the laws of physics would seem to bear me out. As waves rise, they must compress the air above them, causing an increase in air density that could conceivably carry the birds effortlessly up and over the waves.

All species of shearwaters have enlarged nares at the tops of their bills. These nares, which gave rise to the name "tubenoses" for this order of birds, serve to expel excess salt concentrated in large glands above the eyes.

Salt-elimination mechanisms are essential to the survival of pelagic animals, for fresh water is obtainable only through metabolized fats and body fluids from their food, and some direct intake of seawater is unavoidable. The key to water balance in dolphins may be kidneys that can concentrate and excrete large quantities of salt, but this is not known for certain.

The greater shearwaters seen today by the dolphins have flown all the way from the South Atlantic. From here they will continue working their way easterly to Nova Scotia and thence across the North Atlantic to the European coast. In September, they will return the way they came, migrating back to their breeding grounds on remote South Atlantic islands of the Tristan group. On their annual round trip, they cover well over 10,000 miles.

Long, narrow wings enable shearwaters to penetrate winds that send broad-winged birds such as gulls scudding helplessly downwind. Shearwaters often rest in flight, gliding in place against the wind. They are also known to sleep on the surface, heads tucked beneath their wings, so the airborne rest periods may represent light naps. Most shearwaters are accomplished divers, using both their wings and their feet to propel themselves underwater at several knots.

As the young female swam between her mother and nanny, she eyed each humpback they passed, hoping to see the one with the sticklike mark on his flukes. Of all the great whales they had encountered, he had been the most playful.

A large shape materialized ahead and to her left. She swung under her mother to get a better look, and to her astonishment, saw a shark the size of a large orca. From the conical snout to the tip of the great caudal fin, the animal was nearly thirty feet long. She darted back into place, expecting the herd to take quick evasive action, but the dolphins passed nonchalantly within twenty feet of the great beast, which was floating with its back awash.

As the dolphins passed, the shark began slowly sweeping its caudal fin. With its snout projecting above the surface, the shark opened a mouth so cavernous that a harbor seal could have curled up inside with room to spare, and loafed through a swarm of krill and copepods. The young female glanced back and noticed that the shark appeared toothless. Could this be a baby? If so, how big were the adults? Did she envision its mother, larger than a finback whale, lurking somewhere nearby, and shudder?

———~~~~~———

The young dolphin has nothing to fear, for this is a basking shark, second largest of the extant shark species and, like its larger cousin the whale shark, a harmless plankton-eater. To the uninitiated, the basking shark bears a chilling resemblance to that most feared of the mackerel sharks, the great white, but its teeth are less than a quarter-inch long. It subsists entirely on small crustaceans and other planktonic animals, which it sifts from the sea with its gill-rakers. Basking sharks are named for their habit of loafing about at the surface, sometimes with their backs awash, other times floating belly up or on their sides. They appear to enjoy basking in the sun.

Over-fished for their liver oil long ago, and always an easy target for thoughtless or unknowledgeable harpooners, basking sharks are a fairly rare sight in the Gulf of Maine. In July 1982, I saw one over Jeffreys Ledge, thirty miles east of Newburyport. The animal was twenty to twenty-five feet long. It appeared to be sculling its tail very slowly, holding itself stationary against a tidal current. The shark may have been smelling the signs sweeping past it on the current, trying to locate a swarm of krill, which were abundant in the area that day.

From somewhere behind the dolphins and to their left, a heavy booming sound rolled past them, reverberating between bottom and surface like the pealing of distant thunder. At intervals of a minute or two, the sound was repeated again and again.

The leaders turned and headed toward the source of

the sound. In so doing, they cut directly across the path of the basking shark, passing so close to the yawning mouth that the young female could see the animal's gullet. She and the other sucklings shied away, but the shark simply continued to plod along at the surface, mouth agape, seemingly oblivious to their passing. The young female was still uneasy over the proximity of the basking shark. As her learning process developed, though, she would learn which sharks to ignore and which to fear.

A brief, brisk swim brought the dolphins within sight of four humpback whales, who were breaching one after another along a ragged half-mile line. Immediately, the elders began a game that at first had the sucklings hanging back, puzzled and timid. As each whale broke the surface at the beginning of its leap, the dolphins converged on it and arrived just as the animal was crashing back into the water. The impact of each whale's re-entry stunned many sand lances and other small fish, and the dolphins were able to scoop them up by the droves. They moved from one whale to another, sometimes so bent on reaching stunned fish before they recovered their senses, that they darted into re-entry waves only moments after the whales struck the surface.

Each whale breached about twenty times. Then the activity tapered off and stopped, but the dolphins had filled their stomachs with minimum effort, and so regrouped and settled down to nap.

This activity was described to me by Scott Mercer, Director of New Hampshire Whale Watch, Inc. Scott did not see the dolphins actually eating stunned fish—that is pure speculation on my part—but he agreed that it seemed a logical explanation for the animals' behavior.

That same month (July 1982), Scott saw a humpback whale breach 103 consecutive times over Jeffreys Ledge. He said that this marked a new world record for consecutive breachings by a single whale.

A hot, hazy August afternoon, the air so hushed and heavy that it pressed the sea flat. The young female white-side found herself surfacing more frequently than usual, sometimes having to take an extra breath to extract sufficient oxygen from the humid air. The dolphins made few deep dives that afternoon, despite whispery pulses of sound that signaled the presence of short-finned squid hunting far below them.

The setting sun hung bloated in the haze, a great bloody sac, slowly sinking out of sight. Gulls by the thousands winged lazily shoreward, following the twilight toward their island roosts.

The calm persisted until shortly before dark; then sudden wind gusts shivered the surface as a squall line loomed to the northeast. Still miles away but closing fast, lightning walked the sea on crooked legs, its thunderous footsteps sending tremors through the young female white-side. Because sound travels five times faster through water than through air, each lightning bolt that struck the sea was heard twice by the dolphins, first as a sharp crack reverberating through the water, then seconds later as a protracted boom rolling through the air above them.

Each time the young female surfaced, she glanced toward the storm front. Although the sun was no longer visible from sea level, its red glow still highlighted the cloud mass boiling miles into the sky. The bottom of the clouds were flattened and black, the air and sea beneath them deep purple, the darting tentacles of lightning a pale blue violet. Seen through a brief gap in the clouds, the moon appeared to be sailing swiftly north.

The wind keened out of the northeast, opposing a strongly moon-sucked tide and bunching the surface into high choppy waves, then tearing away the wave tops in ragged tatters of spume that smoked the air white with spindrift. Soon the waves were leaping fifteen and twenty feet into the air. The young female found herself sometimes surfacing in deep troughs, at other times soaring high on the crests, looking down at her friends as they skimmed the steep slopes.

Quickly, the storm moved closer. Lightning lanced into the sea. Thunder rolled across the waves. The herd began diving deep and staying down for as long as the sucklings could hold their breath, about five to seven minutes. Sometimes the young female was tossed about at the surface and had trouble effecting a thorough exchange of air, but despite aching lungs and sparks of color flashing against her mental screen, she endured each long submergence. Better that than to surface alone with lightning striking all around her.

After thirty minutes, the lightning abated. With the storm reduced to high winds, the dolphins relaxed and began body-surfing down the slopes of waves. The little ones squealed with delight and forgot their fear altogether. When sliding down long wave slopes with the adults, they found that storms can assume very tolerable proportions.

As night fell, the overcast thinned to closely spaced patches of gray cloud, scudding southwesterly at twenty knots and revealing brief glimpses of the moon between them. The waves continued to run high all night, and the dolphins spent much of the darkness in play, body-surfing the slopes of waves and leaping across their valleys.

An occasional finback passed near them, gliding slickly through the bottoms of waves, breathing in the troughs, its blows rising tall and straight until seized by the wind and scattered like spindrift. The dolphins saw no humpbacks until a few hours before dawn, when three of them broke water about twenty yards away. The whales rolled, puffing on the surface for a time, then sharply arched their backs and sounded, displaying their flukes three-across along the crest of a wave as they slowly slipped out of sight.

The clouds moved on, the wind subsided, and the sea settled into an easy rhythm that lulled the dolphins to sleep. They circled in the moonlight, nursing and napping. Now and again, a muted click-whistle utterance broke the quiet. Dolphin small talk? Or were some of them vocalizing in their sleep? From somewhere far to the east came the dull whump of a whale breaching. Five times the animal leaped and struck the water, then another whale was heard breaching to the north. The two animals continued to breach for a total of more than sixty times between them, then the sounds stopped as suddenly as they had begun. For a time, the only sound was the slow, silken suspiration of the waves.

First light broke with a piercing clarity; no gradual diffusion of color, but a sudden upwelling of golden light at the horizon. One moment the sky overhead was a very deep blue, the stars still clearly visible. Then, the next time the young dolphin looked up, the stars had been replaced by the snowy undersides of gulls on their breakfast flights.

From somewhere out of the depths, the bloated carcass of a young harbor seal rose and broke the surface about fifty feet from the dolphins. Moments later, scores of herring gulls dropped from the sky and descended on the corpse. A loud squabble ensued as the birds fought over the carrion. One of the adult male dolphins reared back and stared at the gulls for a moment, then slipped quietly into the depths.

Moments later, the gulls swimming on the perimeter of the noisy circle cocked their heads and looked down into the water. They paddled this way and that, making *kek-kek-kek* sounds as though uncertain whether to leave or continue pressing for their share of the harbor seal. One by one, they quietly took to the air. The gulls closest to the carcass lingered long enough to snatch a few more morsels, then suddenly exploded into the air, screeching and striking their wings against each other as they scrambled to gain altitude.

From out of the sea below them rocketed the dolphin. The gulls frantically clawed the air with their wings as the big male soared ten, fifteen, nearly twenty feet above the surface. He closed his jaws on the tail of one hapless gull and came away with two long feathers, then jackknifed his body and cleanly re-entered the water head first.

The gulls circled overhead, screeching and defecating in anger. The one with the missing tailfeathers seemed a bit unsteady in its turns, but was otherwise unharmed. It circled with the others, screeching and occasionally swooping toward the dolphins, but staying well clear.

The dolphin floated belly up with the two tailfeathers projecting from his mouth. As though taunting the gulls, he made an *eck-eck-eck* sound, but in so doing, opened his mouth and dropped the feathers. Two females snatched them up, and the three dolphins streaked through the sea, playing steal-the-feather. Then everyone in the herd joined the chase. Leaping, diving, pursuing each other in high speed circles, they continued the game until all that remained of the feathers was a few broken pieces of quill.

Never had the young female enjoyed herself so much with all the adults. Even the three elders who usually led the herd joined in the game.

After a brief rest, the dolphins set off on a somewhat late dawn hunt. There was little surface activity, so they dove and began sweeping the bottom in a parabolic formation, and the firstborn female noticed that it took less time than usual for them to reach the bottom.

Their formation flushed a school of young mackerel, but the fish hugged the rocky bottom, maneuvering through gaps too small for the dolphins to enter. At one point, the fish hid in a narrow gorge, but the dolphins drove them out with pulses of sound so intense that some fish seemed stunned and were easily caught, though most escaped, and the chase continued.[2] Wherever the bottom offered cover, the school diffused, flowed among the rocks like so many living streams, then recombined where the cover thinned. These tinkers had learned well the lessons taught by their first year of survival.

Never before had the young female been able to see the ocean bottom, but now she could. The depth was still great enough to cast a perpetual gloom, but she could make out the silhouettes of dark rocks against white sand.

The dolphins finally managed to trap the school over an open sandy stretch, and caught their fill. It had been a long dive. The sucklings were aching for air.

The young female lay panting in the sunlight beside her mother, glad of the chance to rest and relieve the strain in her lungs. It was pleasant here. The surface was free of chop, but the normally long ocean swells were higher and more closely bunched than usual. Their rise and fall caused a pleasant giddy sensation.

A distant boom turned her attention westerly. She looked, mewed in surprise, and reared back in the water to bring her binocular vision into play. Less than a mile away, waves were thundering against towering cliffs of granite, hurling white water halfway up the sheer slopes. Atop the cliffs were great trees, some of them nearly as high again as the cliffs.

She spun herself around with her flippers and looked north. The cliffs extended as far as she could see. She looked south. A few hundred yards in that direction, the massive rock formations fell away to a strip of white sand that curved half a mile or more to another rocky height. Creatures of some sort were moving about on the sand.

Never had she viewed such wonders. Once, she had seen a small rocky island awash in the swells, one part high enough to provide roosting space for a few dozen gulls and cormorants, but never this much of the ocean bottom rising completely into the air. Here was a world above the sea! She squealed excitedly, trying to get her mother's attention.

Hearing her squeals, the other sucklings swam over to her. Bobbing in the swells like seven little nun buoys set in a row, the youngsters stared at the shoreline. The mothers swam over to them, glanced toward shore, and begun pushing their babies seaward. For the first time, the little ones resisted their mothers' wishes. They squealed and looked back toward the coast. One, the firstborn female, even eluded her mother and swam a short distance toward the cliffs. The other sucklings tried to follow her, but were restrained by their mothers. Now three yearlings ventured shoreward. The adults hung back, but their persistence seemed to be waning. Finally, and with apparent reluctance, they permitted the sucklings to venture toward shore.

The firstborn female took the lead until she was within a half-mile of the cliffs, then waited until her mother and nanny were alongside before starting ahead again. She approached to within a quarter-mile, and stopped. Even from here, the little dolphin could feel the insurge and backsuck of the sea as it assaulted the cliffs. She turned to make sure that her mother was close behind, then moved toward the sandy beach.

At the point where the cliffs fell away to sea level, smoothly sculpted rocks dotted the beach. Countless pebbles, striking against each other in the surge, sounded so much like dolphins echo-clicking that the young female reared back, expecting to see another white-side herd. As her head cleared the water, another sound was borne to her on the wind. It was much like the distant barking she occasionally heard when the dolphins passed within audible range of harbor seals. Then she heard cries like those made by the creatures aboard whale-watching vessels. Soaring high on a wave, she saw a number of them running along the water's edge. Loping alongside two of them was a four-legged animal with golden fur, and it was this one that made the barking sound. The four-legged animal circled the runners, leaping and snapping its jaws in what appeared to be playful behavior.

The other dolphins joined the firstborn, bobbing in the waves a few hundred yards from the beach to watch the joggers and their dog. One of the runners dove into the water and swam parallel to shore, raising his arms high out of the water with each stroke. It was a strange way to swim, but the fact that the creature swam at all made it seem less alien than the ones running on the sand. The firstborn female wanted to examine the swimmer up close, but dared not venture near the surf.

She studied the heights overlooking the beach, where houses with straight sides, pointed corners, and shiny patches, reflected the morning sun. Two of the shore creatures left one of the houses and entered an automobile, which then moved swiftly out of sight. An aircraft droned high overhead. She watched its vapor trail, a long, thin cloud unlike any cloud she had seen before. Such things fascinated her, but her curiosity was tinged with fear.

Sinking below the surface, she heard water surging, bubbles bursting, and thrusting her head back into the air, she looked to the south. Nothing was visible, but the sounds continued. She dove and moved slowly toward the sound, swinging her head from side to side, centering on the source with the directional oil-filled hearing canal inside her lower jaw. Something was swimming out there, and judging by its surface surge, it was about the size of a dolphin, but was moving quite slowly. She paused and looked back. The other sucklings were following her, and the adults were just behind them. Drawing courage from their presence, she surfaced and took several deep breaths, then dove deep and swam toward the sound. A sense of adventure tingled along her spine.

Soon the sounds were coming from nearly overhead. She rolled over, looked up, and saw a man swimming on his back about a hundred yards from shore. She and the others circled twenty feet below him.

Unlike the first swimmer, this one was not raising his arms high out of the water. As he spread his legs wide and snapped them together, he swept his arms down along his sides like a humpback thrusting with its flippers, then glided with legs together and arms against his sides. On the return stroke, he brought his arms back along his chest, keeping them against his body to minimize drag, while spreading his legs in preparation for the next power stroke.

A considerable chop had been building since the dolphins approached shore, but the swimmer's use of the elementary backstroke enabled him to knife through the bottoms of the waves and maintain a brisk pace. He breathed in the wave troughs, blowing the water clear of his mouth and quickly inhaling before the next wave covered his face. His breathing sounded so much like a dolphin's that the young female no longer felt afraid. Slowly, she rose to within ten feet of the swimmer, then rolled onto her back so that she could watch him with both eyes.

She heard the faint whine of a distant motorboat. Moments later, the swimmer treaded water and looked around, then changed to a breaststroke so that he could watch for the boat. The sound of high-speed propellers grew louder. Soon the firstborn dolphin could hear the hollow thump of the boat's hull bouncing across the waves. The swimmer stopped and kicked himself high in the water, waving his arms and shouting, then took several deep breaths and dove.

Taken by surprise, the young female hesitated. The man spotted her, changed direction, and leveled off about ten feet away from her, holding himself down with upward sweeps of his arms. Wide-eyed with surprise and fear, man and dolphin stared at each other for a moment. Then she turned and followed the others toward deeper water.

After the motorboat roared overhead and passed clear, the man surfaced and wiped the brine from his eyes. The pallor of fear added a gray tinge to his tanned face. He glanced down into the water, then turned and looked all around him. A hundred yards seaward, small puffs of spray appeared above the wave tops, and he heard the chuffs of the dolphins' exhalations. He smiled, shook his head, and continued his swim.

The young female was about a hundred yards behind the other dolphins, who had paused to wait for her, when the motorboat returned and made a high-speed run between her and the herd. Frightened by the piercing whine of the outboard motor, she swung left and went deep, heading away from the boat. The other dolphins, also frightened by the boat, raced directly out to sea. Within a minute, the distance between the young female and the others had opened to a mile or more, and was further increasing with each passing second.

Having seen dorsal fins break the surface, the young man at the helm of the boat circled the area, revving the engine and shouting to his girl friend that he saw sharks.

Confused by the shrill propeller noise, which seemed to be coming from all directions as the boat circled, the young dolphin inadvertently surfaced for air directly in the boat's path. She glimpsed white water leaping either side of the sharp prow, then quickly sucked air into her aching lungs and dove. The engine snarled as the boy spotted her and accelerated. She just barely avoided being slashed by the propeller as she headed for the bottom.

Although her time at the surface was brief and stressful, she had noticed as she dove that she was angling back toward the beach, so she turned and headed into deeper water. As the depth increased, the bottom became less and less visible. Fearing collision, she was forced to slow her pace. The next time she popped to the surface, the shoreline was half a mile away, and the boat was still circling the same general area.

Only now, with the immediate danger behind her, did she suddenly realize how far away the other dolphins must be. She was lost! So terrifying was the thought that she gave vent to it with the first full-blown whistle she had ever managed to produce. Again she whistled, and again, hoping her mother would hear her. Between whistles, she listened for a response, but all she could hear was the shrill *zeeeee* of another high-speed motorboat approaching from her left. She filled her lungs and dove.

Thirty feet down, she leveled off and continued swimming directly out to sea. The boat passed safely clear, but she maintained her depth and continued to sound her distress whistle. Her whistles saved her from what might have been a serious collision, for she suddenly heard a whistle echo and pulled up just in time to avoid a large rock. Her flukes scraped the barnacled outcropping, but she escaped serious injury.

The shock of the near collision temporarily displaced her fear of solitude, and brought to mind something she had noticed while following her guardians during hunts. Often, as the adults dove toward the bottom in pursuit of fish, she heard clicking sounds from ahead as well as from the dolphins on either side of her. She recalled thinking that it sounded as though other dolphins were approaching them from ahead, and it had always puzzled her when the approaching dolphins never materialized. She also recalled that the adults usually maneuvered to either side when they heard these sounds coming from ahead of them, much as she had done when she heard her whistle reflected from the rock. That must be why the adults were continually clicking or whistling, to avoid bumping into things. Until she was alone, she had never had to do it.

It was a small step for her young mind to conclude that the adults must also use echoes to locate and catch their food, for they vocalized more than ever during hunts. Still, they seemed to use clicks more than whistles when hunting or maneuvering along the bottom, and she did not even know how to make a clicking sound. Whistles were easy; she merely constricted her nasal passages and forced air back and forth through her nasal sacs. What must she do to make clicking sounds?

As she continued slowly seaward, doing her best to stay halfway between surface and bottom, she experimented with various sounds, and became so engrossed in her search for a proper click that she nearly forgot her fear of being separated from the others. At length, by pressing her tongue against the roof of her mouth and forcing brief bursts of air from her throat into her nasal sacs, she produced a sound similar to the clicks used by the adults. Although unaware of the mechanisms involved, she could feel a membrane or valve somewhere within her nasal passages snapping with increasing vigor as she practiced the procedure. After forcing bursts of air into her nasal sacs for ten to twenty seconds, she built up so much back pressure that she could not make a sound, but she soon discovered that she could reduce the pressure by swallowing.

Before long, the snapping mechanism in her nasal passages was producing fairly crisp pulses of sound, and she was gradually able to increase the intensity of the sound to the point where she was receiving clearly audible echoes from the bottom. Although crude in comparison to the adults' precisely controlled click-bursts, the sounds were a dramatic improvement over her whistles. The pulsed sound was sharper, more directional than whistles, far better for detecting individual bottom formations.

Hearing solid, sharp echoes from directly ahead, she reduced speed and swung her head from side to side. The echoes persisted well to either side, but when she tilted her head upward, the echoes faded. Swinging her head alternately upward and downward, then from side to side, she slowly ascended and found herself passing over a fairly steep bank that rose to within twenty feet of the surface.

The sun was now nearly overhead, and as it cleared a patch of dense white cloud, the young dolphin could see the shallow bottom reasonably well. This enabled her to make visual confirmations of her acoustic hits and misses. Staying close to the bottom, she continued to echo-navigate her way seaward, learning as she went how the echoes varied depending on object size, solidity, and range. She surfaced for air every few minutes, but each time returned to the bottom, where she was safe from passing vessels.

Swimming steadily out to sea, she learned more with each passing minute. For long-range detection, she used widely spaced pulses of maximum intensity. When she began receiving echoes from a distant object, she ''illuminated'' it with more closely spaced pulses to get some idea how large it was and how far across her path it extended. As she approached closer, she further increased her click rate to a buzzing sound and swung her head to scan the object, gaining a better idea of its size and shape.

This matter of scanning objects was essential, but when swimming at anything more than dead slow speed, she found that head movements changed her direction and disrupted her orientation. If only there were some way she could swing the sound beam without moving her head. Again, through trial and error, she found that by inflating various sacs, she could change the shape of the oil-filled chamber inside her forehead, thereby skewing her sound beams without swinging her head and throwing herself off course. Also, she could hear her sound beam broaden as she lowered the transmission frequency, and become narrower as she increased the frequency. By changing the frequency, she could vary her sound beam from a "floodlight" to a "spotlight."[3]

By repeatedly confirming her acoustic hunches with visual observations, she was soon learning to distinguish the sharp echoes of rocks from the softer echoes of vegetation and large bottom fish. Her technique remained crude, and miscalculations cost her a few painful scrapes, but she was learning, and the flood of new knowledge excited her.

About two miles from the beach, she began receiving mushy echoes from something ahead of her, and noted that the buzz tone of the echoes sounded higher than that of her outgoing clicks. She learned why moments later when a vast school of mackerel parted just ahead and flowed around her. The mackerel school had provided her first lesson in Doppler shift. In time, she would come to understand that sound contacts moving toward her cause an upward shift in echo pitch, while those moving away cause a downward shift.

The young dolphin shuddered with excitement. Until now, she had been able to hear in the passive sense only, and was completely dependent on the guidance of others when swimming in dark waters. She still had a great deal to learn, and would not become totally proficient for a year or two, but necessity had forced her to take a quantum leap in the learning process.

Another upshift echo from ahead. She constricted her nasopharyngeal passages and produced the most closely spaced train of clicks thus far, then tried to guess what lay ahead. Another school of fish? Perhaps, but this contact sounded a bit more solid, its echoes less scattered than those from the mackerel school. Now the echoes faded to a whisper, but increased their upshift. Puzzled, she turned to bring her eyes into play, and found herself on a collision course with a snaggle-toothed brown shark half again as long as she was. Whipping her body into a tight turn, she darted back the way she had come, and nearly collided with her mother and nanny, who had been following about fifty yards behind her for some time. Seeing itself outnumbered, the brown shark slipped out of sight.

The young female was overjoyed to see her mother and nanny, but their sudden appearance puzzled her. Had they been following her all along, and if so, why had they not answered her calls for help much sooner? Years later, when she had her first baby, she would un-

115

derstand that youngsters best learn the lessons of survival when forced to fend for themselves.

She rubbed against her mother and nanny, expressing with whistles and clicks her joy at being reunited with them. Within moments, the surprisingly self-sufficient young dolphin had reverted to the totally dependent baby and was hungrily seeking her mother's mammary glands.

Not once during the next two days did she leave her mother's side.

Six

THE FIRSTBORN FEMALE'S sudden discovery of her phonation apparatus created quite a stir among the other sucklings, none of whom could as yet manage more than an occasional peep or bleat. When they heard her clicking and whistling nearly as well as the yearlings, the sucklings crowded around and pressed their beaks against her, as they might if a young stranger had appeared in their midst.

More keenly attuned now to the phonations of the adults, the young female listened closely and tried to mimic them as the herd navigated and hunted. In the course of this, she found that every sound she made had a unique voice, which she could single out from among the babble of echoes returning to the herd. The importance of this soon became clear to her. Each dolphin transmitted sound in a different way for a different purpose, however slight, even during cooperative ventures such as hunts, so the returning echoes had different meanings for various individuals. Were she unable to discriminate her echoes from the others, she would be totally confused.

Her knowledge and skill increased daily. Until now, she had been clicking in bursts, waiting for her echoes to return before sending out another burst. As a result, she had often failed to sense important changes of state that occurred during her silent periods, and she was unprepared for sudden herd maneuvers. The adults, on the other hand, seemed able to analyze their echoes while clicking continuously. One day, she mimicked her mother's variations in click rate, and noticed that the adult spaced her pulses so that the incoming echoes could slip in between the outgoing clicks. The transmitted pulses were always louder than the echoes, so she had no trouble distinguishing between them. Even if they were equal in strength, she could distinguish between them, for the clicks were transmitted primarily through her forehead, whereas the returning echoes were channeled most loudly through her lower jaw.

After a few days of practice, she became fairly adept at varying her click rate for optimum echo clarity. The interleaving of transmitted and received pulses was fairly easy with distant contacts, because for long-range soundings, she had to use lower pulse rates so that she could make each click loud enough to reach the target and return an audible echo. At shorter ranges and higher pulse rates, though, phasing was a bit more critical, so she simply swept her click rate higher and lower until she heard the echoes most clearly.

The noise and frantic pace of hunts still confused her, so she took every opportunity to practice by herself. Often, as the herd sleep-circled, she would venture a short distance away and conduct solo explorations. One day, as usual, she started by scanning the area with loud, widely spaced snaps for long-range detection. As she began picking up audible echoes, she analyzed them. How far away was the thing? The greater the distance, the longer it took for her echoes to return. As the range closed, she scanned the contact with more closely spaced pulses to gain some idea of the thing's size, bearing in mind that a distant whale scans no larger than a fairly close shark. Did the echoes sound hard, like those from a rock? No, they sounded slightly mushy, like the echoes from a living thing. Which way was the thing moving? No upshift or downshift, merely a change of bearing from left to right; the thing seemed to be circling the herd at a constant distance. She moved toward the contact, scanning it at a pulse rate so high that her clicks made a buzzing sound. Although still a fair swim away, the thing scanned as large as a whale, but was not shaped like one. She concluded that it must be a school of fish, and swam closer to get a visual confirmation.

To her surprise, the contact proved to be a solitary right whale, but what she saw was quite different from what she heard. Her pulses of sound were not being reflected from the whale as a whole, but primarily from the whale's lungs and other air-filled body cavities. The rest of a whale's body is about the same density as the surrounding water, and so, is largely transparent to sound. She later observed that this was the case with all animals she echo-scanned, including other dolphins. Never again would she confuse large animals such as whales with schools of fish, for although a fish school may be as large as a whale, it produces many small ech-

119

oes from the individual fishes' swim bladders, whereas a whale sounds like a few large returns.

One important aid to the young dolphin's survival is the use of Doppler shift to determine whether contacts are closing on her or moving away. To do this, her brain must not only interlace outgoing pulses and incoming echoes, but must simultaneously analyze the relative click rates or buzz tones of the two. Fortunately, nature has provided her with a built-in superheterodyne receiver for this purpose. When the buzz tone of the incoming echoes varies from that of the outgoing pulses, she hears a lower beat tone, which is the difference between the first two. When the beat tone increases, it signals that she and the contact are closing on each other. Knowing the Doppler shift imposed by her own speed on echoes from stationary objects ahead, she can then estimate the speed of the closing contact, relative to hers. When the beat tone swings lower, she knows that the distance between her and the contact is increasing.

It is all too much for the youngster to master in such a short time, but she does manage to gain a rough idea of the relative speed and direction of movement for various creatures she detects.

While trying to master the use of Doppler shift, she also learned an important secondary use of the dolphins' whistle-calls. Each dolphin has a distinctly different whistle, and the young female had known for some time that the calls served to identify various members of the herd, but now she discovered that the whistles could also be used for omnidirectional detection.

When the young dolphin transmitted pulses, she knew from experience that the sound was propagated in a fairly narrow beam ahead of her. If she had been forced to rely on pulsed sound to guard against attack from all directions, she would have spent most of her time swimming in circles. This was where the whistle-call came into play, for it was not focused ahead of her, but propagated in all directions. Lately, as she developed her whistle to a clear, high-intensity sound wave, she noticed its echo returning faintly from various directions and with varying Doppler shifts. As she swam at a given speed, the whistle echoes from the ocean bottom and other stationary objects ahead of her were shifted upward in pitch, while those from objects falling away behind her were down-shifted.

One day, a large shark came up behind the herd, and started gaining swiftly on the dolphins. Immediately, the young female heard her whistle echo from the rear being upshifted, making the presence of the shark stand out from among the downshifted background echoes. Much to the credit of this suckling, she was among the first to turn and point out the danger with a burst of sharp pulses.

Though she still had much to learn, the sense of discovery and growing self-sufficiency enabled her to assume a role other than dependency.

Despite extensive postmortem anatomical studies and tank experiments with live animals, the sound-production mechanisms of dolphins are poorly understood, but scientists have reached certain generally accepted conclusions. It appears that the animals produce sound in their nasal passages rather than in their

121

larynges. (They have no vocal cords.) The prevailing hypothesis suggests that sound is produced by means of nasal plug nodes, diagonal membranes, and nasofrontal sacs—the latter perhaps acting as resonators while the large vestibular sacs serve as air reservoirs.[1]

Two types of sound are produced: pulses (clicks) and continuous waves (whistles). Clicks appear to be transmitted directionally through the oil-filled acoustical "melon" in the head, whereas whistles are omnidirectional. The most sensitive directional channel for sound reception is through the oil-filled lower jawbone. (The oil conducts sound with far lower loss than other parts of the body.) Thus, a dolphin can swing its head or lobe-switch its "antenna patterns" by distorting its "melon," and can pinpoint sound sources to accuracies of a few degrees. The animals also have oil-filled acoustical "windows" on both sides of their skulls at the base of the lower jaw, together with smaller ones just above the flippers. These are probably used for passive detection of sounds coming from either side. By sensing arrival-time differences, the animals may be able to determine the direction of such sounds, then turn toward them to make active echo-surveillances.[2]

External ears such as ours are useless for determining the direction of underwater sounds, because when submerged, our ears conduct sound no better than the rest of our bodies. For this reason, together with evolutionary pressures toward hydrodynamic streamlining, dolphins have no external ears. A dolphin's ear meatuses are threadlike wax-filled canals that terminate as pinholes at either side of the head. They are largely vestigial, and according to published test results, are no more sound-sensitive than the rest of the animal's head. Dolphins do seem to hear airborne sounds quite well, but they may do so through their oil-filled acoustic windows rather than through their ear holes.

Experimental data suggest that dolphins may have two separate acoustic subsystems: one for lower-frequency passive hearing and another for higher-frequency active hearing (echolocation). A dolphin's collicular (midbrain) acoustic response shows high selectivity for the onset of steeply rising sound bursts (high-frequency response), is much less sensitive to slow rise times, and is nearly insensitive to maintained (continuous) sound. This sensitivity to rate of rise is combined with the ability to discriminate among different frequencies even in very brief tones, and in the first fraction of a millisecond of longer tones. Such appears to be the key to a dolphin's ability to discriminate ultrasonic clicks.

It appears that lower-frequency, slowly rising signals such as whistles, could not be processed in a dolphin's colliculus (midbrain). Rather, it is thought that such signals are processed at higher levels, presumably in the cerebral cortex. This hypothesis ties in with the prevailing view that dolphins' whistles are used primarily for social communications.

Many cetologists, adhering to the view that the animals' whistles are used exclusively for social communications, rule out the possibility that they might also be used for detection. With all due respect, it seems more plausible to me that the whistles serve both purposes. A dolphin's pulsed sounds are propagated in a directional beam ahead of the animal. Unless the animal had an omnidirectional active detection device such as the Doppler whistle sonar suggested in the preceding scene (and suggested earlier by John C. Lilly and others), how would it know when silent predators were approaching from the rear?

As for the social communication function of whistles, would it not make sense for the animals to carry out such communications in ultrasound, at least over short distances? Ultrasonic whistles would be inaudible to most of their predators, yet dolphins are heard emitting sonic whistles continually while on the move, and it appears that they repeat the same whistles time and again. It may be that these are signature whistles, used merely to keep track of each other's positions, but they could do this ultrasonically with far greater security.

All things considered, it seems more logical to me that these whistles (1) identify individuals, (2) provide omnidirectional Doppler surveillance, and (3) provide longer-range detection than could be achieved with ultrasonic whistles.

Another topic open to speculation is the means by which dolphins determine the distance to various objects and creatures. Many scientists believe that time separation pitch (TSP) is the key to this. A train of clicks transmitted by a dolphin produces an apparent tone, ranging from a creaking sound for lower pulse repetition rates (PRR) to a buzz for intermediate PRR to a fairly high-pitched whine for high PRR. The interaction of the outgoing tone with that of the returning echoes may produce a beat-tone, the way two tuning forks vibrating at different frequencies can cause us to hear a third tone equal to the sum of or difference between the original frequencies.[3]

In the preceding scene, the young dolphin was using the difference frequency beat-tone to determine whether contacts were closing or moving away. (The extended hearing range of dolphins may enable them to use the sum frequency beat-tones, as well.) She was not using TSP to determine range. That would probably require far more experience than she had. A dolphin would have to know from past observations which TSP beat-tones are produced by contacts at various ranges.

In actuality, a dolphin may never need to know the precise distance to a sound contact. Although, with practice, the animals may be able to determine range quite accurately, they can probably get by in most instances with a rough idea of the distance. More important, it seems to me, is for them to know how quickly and in which direction the distance is changing. The round-trip travel time of a single pulse should provide a fairly accurate indication of range. With sufficient practice in this sort of thing, a dolphin must develop a fair degree of skill through visual confirmations of acoustic guesses.

As for direction and rate of range change, the dolphin need simply listen for changes in the beat-tone. If the dolphin is clicking at a fixed PRR and the contact is closing, the returning pulses will be more tightly bunched than they were when transmitted. Thus, the received PRR will be higher than the transmitted PRR, thereby increasing the TSP to a higher tone. This tells the dolphin that it and the contact are closing on each other. The rate at which the TSP increases gives the dolphin some idea of closing speed. Knowing its own speed and, from experience, the TSP that a given speed produces from fixed objects such as the ocean bottom, the dolphin can estimate the speed of the approaching contact.

Between transmitted pulses, dolphins appear to allow intervals three to twenty milliseconds longer than the time required for a pulse to reach the "target" and return to sender. One purpose of this may be range determination. The intervals between outgoing pulses may also help avoid interference with incoming echoes.

It would seem, then, that the animals wish to receive and process each echo before transmitting the next pulse, but beyond ranging on a contact with a single "snap" sort of pulse, it is doubtful that a dolphin dwells on each echo. More likely, the animal integrates many echoes and merely processes the periodic changes of state, much as we do with visual images. Our visual sensory systems are continually responding to the intensity, motion, color, shape, and triangulation (range) of images reaching our retinas. Although we occasionally concentrate on individual characteristics such as lovely colors, we generally integrate the various sensory data and base our decisions on overall impressions. Similarly, a dolphin's acoustical senses respond to the intensity (loudness), motion (Doppler shift), acoustic color (amplitude/phase distortions), shape (scan "image"), and range (round-trip travel time or TSP) of the reflected sounds reaching its inner ears. Experienced animals probably base their decisions on overall acoustical impressions.

This sight-sound analogy is valid enough. The dolphin's ability to process acoustical information is on a par with our capabilities in processing visual information. Detection and differentiation appear to take place in the animal's colliculus, while the higher order functions of integration, analysis, and decision-making are most likely performed in the cerebral cortex.

Hearing has become the dominant sense among cetaceans because underwater visibility is so limited, but how do the animals cope with hearing limitations such as high ambient noise levels? The sounds made by other creatures, waves, and propellers combine to create a clutter that might very well make it impossible to detect meaningful sounds.

Dolphins avoid most of this interference by tuning above it. Whereas most of their environment's ambient sounds are in the lower range of frequencies (100 to 1,500 cycles per second), the lowest-frequency dolphin phonations are near the upper limits of human hearing, and their highest-frequency phonations extend to at least 208,000 cycles per second.[4] Furthermore, most of the sounds in their acoustical ambience do not involve rapid rise times, so the colliculus, a dolphin's major detection apparatus, is unresponsive to them. Thus, although the dolphin can hear these ambient sounds, process them in its cortex, and take appropriate action, the sounds do not interfere with its active detection and ranging mechanisms.

One form of interference that can cause problems for dolphins is reverberation. Shoal-water dolphins such as the bottlenose *(Tursiops truncatus)* apparently learn to cope with high levels of reverberation. Pelagic species like *Lagenorhynchus acutus*, the principal topic of this book, are less subject to reverberation and may become badly confused should they encounter it. This could be one explanation for the occasional mass strandings of such animals. While pursuing prey or being pursued by predators, they may venture into shoal waters and become disoriented by the high reverberation levels.

As I mentioned earlier, the prevailing theory of sound production in odontocetes (toothed whales) suggests that the animals generate pulsed sounds by snapping tough nasal plugs against bony nares. This theory may soon be displaced by a more likely hypothesis, for no natural muscle or membrane has ever been known to vibrate as fast as a dolphin's higher pulse repetition rates of about 1,200 pulses per second.

One alternative model has the animals using controlled bursts of air to produce pulsed sounds. That they cycle air between their lungs and nasal sacs when phonating is a known fact. The animals may use the larger vestibular sacs as air reservoirs while constricting or expanding the smaller nasofrontal sacs so that they function as tunable resonators. It is also known that their nasal plugs move during phonation, for X-ray motion pictures have shown this clearly. Not so clear is the issue of whether the plugs actually snap against the nares to generate sound and, again, whether they could do so quickly enough to achieve pulse repetition rates as high as 1,200 pulses per second. For the production of whistles, the nasal plugs and bony nares may function like the valves on a flute, varying aperture to control pitch. For the production of pulsed sound, the plug-

128

nare interface may serve somewhat the same purpose as the mouth hole of a flute, splitting the air column against an edge and causing it to vibrate.

The pulsed air concept is at least partially demonstrable with our own nasopharyngeal mechanisms. While thinking about this in my bathtub one day, I submerged my head, held my mouth and nostrils (blowhole) closed, and experimented with various ways of producing sound without using my vocal chords.

First, I tried the technique used by cancer patients who, having lost their larynges, learn to speak by means of controlled belching. This technique produced creaking sounds similar to a dolphin's midrange click rates, but gave me no control over pulse repetition rate.

Next, I tried pressing the back of my tongue against the roof of my mouth and forcing bursts of air past the tongue into my cheeks. Using this technique, I was able to produce fairly loud sounds similar to the grunting of a hog. By pressing my tongue more firmly against the roof of my mouth, I was able to generate trains of clicks. The intensity was nowhere near that of a dolphin's pulses, of course, but it was surprisingly loud when heard under water. After a few practice runs, I found that I could control pulse repetition rate fairly well over a range extending from single snaps to one hundred pulses per second or higher.

I also found that, as my pulsing increased the pressure to the point where air began escaping from mouth or nostrils, I could relieve the pressure by swallowing, then start over again with little time lost. This recirculation of air had a bonus effect in that it substantially increased my submergence time.

Seven

A FEW WEEKS AFTER the white-sided dolphins encountered orcas over the eastern periphery of Jeffreys Ledge, the worst of the tuna fishermen's fears were realized. Their prime bluefin fishing grounds over Jeffreys Ledge and Stellwagen Bank were invaded by orcas.

The first news of orcas in the area comprised several unconfirmed reports of an attack on three finback whales near Jeffreys Ledge. There are no photographs confirming the attack, but Jay Neeland described the event as follows for The Gulf of Maine Whale Sighting Network:

> A group of 40–50 killer whales broke up into three groups as they approached three finback whales. Each group began attacking a different finback. The killer whales dove under the finbacks and bit off pieces of meat, pushing the finbacks up out of the water a little during the attack. Feeding continued for over two hours and when it was over the water was full of pieces of meat and blood. The whales were not observed after the attack. If they were killed, the carcasses would have sunk.

If swift finbacks are as easy targets for mass orca attacks, as this report suggests, it is a wonder that the slower humpbacks are not massacred when orcas visit their feeding grounds. In fact, upward of half the humpbacks seen in the Gulf of Maine do bear long parallel scars, as many as ten across, on their flippers and flukes, and near their dorsal fins. These are not the crisscross scars so typical of propeller wounds, but look more like the sort of scars that would be left by orcas which, like dogs nipping at the heels of horses, reportedly delight in raking humpbacks with their teeth. Many humpbacks are also missing round chunks of flesh ranging from a few inches to a foot in diameter. The larger wounds appear to be shark bites. The smaller ones may be caused by bluefish in their feeding frenzies.

Although finback whales seldom expose more than their backs when surfacing, they appear on average to be far less scarred than humpback whales. This may be due to their speed—they can sprint at about 20 knots—which undoubtedly gives sharks and bluefish few opportunities to sample their flesh. As for orcas, when they exert the effort required to catch finbacks, they probably have more lethal goals in mind than merely raking the whales with their teeth.

Word of the orca pod spread quickly by marine radio, and the tuna fishermen braced themselves for the worst. Might some of the fishermen retaliate if the orcas threatened to drive the bluefins off the banks? Any violent action would seem foolhardy, for anyone harming or harassing marine mammals faces fines up to $20,000, liens against his vessel as high as $25,000, and/or imprisonment for up to one year. Still, each giant bluefin represents thousands of dollars to the fishermen, so emotions could run high.

Early morning. The white-sided dolphins were about ten miles off Rockport, Massachusetts when once again they heard the hunting cries of orcas. For the past hour, the whiteside herd had been hunting in the company of many large bluefin tuna. The young female had enjoyed watching the great fish flash through the water in pursuit of mackerel, but as soon as the orca calls were heard, the bluefins disappeared into the depths. She attempted to echo-click on one bluefin, a giant that must surely have weighed a thousand pounds, but as soon as the fish went deep, its echoes were lost amid bottom clutter. She understood now why the tuna were going deep. It would be difficult for the orcas to detect them while they were close to the bottom. Also, bluefins could stay deep indefinitely, whereas orcas had to surface periodically for air, and in so doing, could lose track of their prey.

A mile east of the dolphins, a dozen sport fishing boats were anchored. The fishing had been good. Already, four fishermen had "hooked on" and one 800-pound bluefin had been boated. Expectations were so high among the fishermen that the orca threat was nearly forgotten.

One team had an eight-foot bluefin close aboard. The gaffer was leaning over the taffrail to secure the

132

catch when a large black and white form flashed out of the depths and struck the tuna, nearly pulling the gaffer over the side. The man in the fighting chair had the heavy rod nearly ripped from his hands, but he managed to ease drag on the reel in time to prevent the line from parting. A hundred yards of line screamed out of the reel, which began to smoke and had to be doused with water. Suddenly, the line went slack. The man reeled in, and the gaffer retrieved what was left of the catch. The bluefin's body had been severed just behind the gills. All that remained was the head, its jaw still snapping in macabre death throes.

A hundred yards astern, a five-foot dorsal fin broke the surface, and a plume of vapor punctuated the morning air. Three shorter fins converged on the first, and the four orcas proceeded to divide the catch among them. The men watched and cursed. Then the skipper cupped his hands to his mouth and spread the word to nearby boats. "Killer whales just stole an eight-hundred-pound bluefin. Spread the word, but don't use your radios." The message was passed from boat to boat.

A quarter-mile from the anchored rod-and-reel fishermen, a solitary sport fishing vessel cruised slowly in a great circle around the other boats. A wiry young man stood in the pulpit, leaning his weight easily against the metal ring encircling him, balancing a long harpoon on his right shoulder. From the barbed head of the harpoon, a stout nylon line ran back to the foredeck, to a carefully coiled reserve of line, the end of which was attached to a large fluorescent orange pennant float.

A flash of white in the water ahead of the boat

133

brought the man to attention. He turned and called up to his mate, seated at the steering station aloft. "Meet her, Larry. Steady as you go." Balancing the harpoon in his right hand, he shaded his eyes and studied the water. Several patches of white, moving as one, were rising slowly toward the surface. Harpoon at the ready, the man planted his feet wide against the roll of a beam swell. The hand gripping the harpoon blanched at the knuckles, trembled slightly, then relaxed again. He lowered the harpoon. "It's a killer, Larry, and I damn near stuck him." The boat passed over the orca, which had apparently seen the harpooner and sounded.

Moments later, the boat moved within hailing distance of one of the anchored vessels, and the men received word of the bluefin catch lost to orcas. While the message was being passed, the men heard angry shouts from a nearby boat as the orcas snatched away another hooked bluefin.

The vessel rigged for harpooning maneuvered among the others, moving from boat to boat as the skippers conferred with each other. The men were of one mind. They were not about to stand by and watch the orcas ruin tens of thousands of dollars' worth of fishing. Small boxes of cherry bombs were distributed among several crews. Then with lookouts maintaining a sharp watch for Coast Guard vessels or aircraft, the men awaited the next attack.

Shortly after hearing orca calls from the north, the dolphins headed southeasterly, apparently wishing to move well clear of shoal waters where they could more easily be trapped by the killer whales. Their first encounter with the orca pod had suggested that the whales were intent on catching bluefins, not dolphins, but they apparently intended to play it safe and stay well clear of their great cousins.

The herd leaders set a surprisingly moderate pace of about ten knots. Were they conserving energy, or did they fear rushing headlong into the very sort of trap they had seen used on the bluefins? If the latter, then their fears were well founded, for they had covered less than a mile when they heard orcas calling from the east and south.

Three contingents of orcas seemed to be making a great sweep of the area, converging on the fishing grounds where the boats were anchored. The dolphin herd leaders paused and exchanged some sort of click-whistle observation, then turned and headed back the way they had come. The young female heard her mother's heartbeat accelerate, and was afraid.

As the white-sides again passed within a mile of the anchored fishing boats, the first group of orcas had already reached the area. The dolphins could hear their heavy clicking sounds as they maneuvered beneath the boats, darting this way and that in pursuit of bluefin tuna. A thud, a whining sound, then the next time the dolphins surfaced, they heard the fishermen shouting angrily. The dolphins turned westerly and headed directly toward land.

Cherry bombs in hand, the fishermen waited for the orcas to show themselves again. Since the theft of the second bluefin, not one of the thirty-odd boats in the area had managed to "hook up," so it appeared that the day's fishing had already been ruined, but the fishermen waited, nonetheless. Given their chance, they might be able to discourage the orcas from hunting there again.

To this point, the fishermen had seen only six or eight orcas, so they were unprepared for the shouts that soon came from lookouts in the vessels' crow's nests.

"Killers. A dozen of them, coming from the south."

"Ten to fifteen killer whales approaching from the east, about a mile out."

Worst of all, for the dolphins, came the cry, "More of them, a mile or two west of us."

Now eight orcas, probably the ones who had been stealing the fishermen's catches, surfaced a hundred yards south of the anchored vessels. As if on cue, the orcas in all directions began breaching and lob-tailing, whipping the surface into a froth and making a thunderous commotion as they continued to close their circle on a central point about half a mile south of the boats. Soon their circle measured less than a mile across, and their concerted breaching sounded like heavy surf breaking on a beach.

Ten of the boat skippers fired up their engines, weighed anchor, and proceeded at high speed toward the orcas. Aboard each vessel, a man stood ready with lighted cigar or cigarette and a boxful of cherry bombs.

As the fishermen approached, the orcas sounded. The men circled and waited for the whales to surface for air, but instead of orcas, they soon saw dozens of giant bluefins flopping about helplessly at the surface, their caudal fins severed. A slick of blood and oil began to sheen the surface, diffracting the sunlight into swirling rainbows.

Now dorsal fins broke the surface, but the lookouts reported that they were merely white-sided dolphins. The dolphins darted this way and that among the boats, giving the men the impression that they were feeding on smaller fish while the orcas hunted the bluefins.

Finally, the orcas surfaced for air, and the men began hurling their cherry bombs.[1]

As the boats approached and lay to, the dolphins swam among them, perhaps hoping that the orcas would not follow. The young female, her mother, nanny, and six other dolphins had just sought refuge beneath one of the boats when the orcas' massive black and white forms began rising out of the depths and breaking the surface. There were the sounds of running feet on the boat above, then suddenly the sea exploded, and the dolphins scattered in total panic.

The next few minutes were a blur of terror and confusion for the young dolphin. She was swimming at top speed, with no idea where she was going. When the explosions started, she and her escorts must have scattered in different directions, for she was now alone.

Breaking the surface for air, she happened to pass within a body length of where a small object struck the water. A deafening explosion sent her darting to the left, and she nearly collided with a twenty-foot orca that was rising for air. She grazed the whale's side, barely avoiding its powerful flukes, and went deep to escape another series of explosions. There were orcas everywhere, and they seemed as confused as she. Deeper and deeper she dove, and only when she heard the scuttling, snapping sounds of frightened lobsters did she remember to use her sonar. As soon as she started clicking, she heard echoes, and pulled up just in time to avoid striking the bottom.

Slowing her pace, she acoustically felt her way along the bottom, not really caring which way she was headed, as long as her course took her away from the surface explosions. Now and then she heard other dolphins buzzing, and tried to intercept them, but was disoriented èach time by another explosion or a close encounter with orcas. At last, she put the chaotic scene behind her and shot to the surface for air.

Dizzy from lack of oxygen, exhausted by her ordeal, the young dolphin lay puffing in the sunshine, whistling plaintively for her mother. She had left the boats about two miles behind her. Six or seven miles ahead, the top of a high rocky promontory was visible. Between whistles, she listened for signs of her mother or other members of the herd. Clicking sounds were faintly audible, but she was not sure whether they came from orcas or dolphins, and the sounds were so widely dispersed that she could not possibly decide which ones to follow. She decided to wait where she was and hope that her mother would hear her calls.

For the second time in two weeks, she was alone. While safe within the herd's formation, she seldom stopped to think about the sea's immensity and hostility. Alone, as now, she felt infinitesimally small and totally vulnerable. Her heart fluttered as if trying to escape her chest. Anxiety, worsened by hunger, twisted her stomach into painful knots.

A stream of clicks, louder than the background sounds, reached her from the direction of the boats. The sound rose, faded, then intensified again, as though she were being scanned by another dolphin. The clicks sounded heavy. She stopped whistling and faced the sound. Might it be one of the herd's largest adults, or was it an orca? Not daring to make a sound, she reared back and thrust herself high out of the water to take a look.

Kawhoosh! A plume of vapor rose above the waves. Scarcely fifty yards away loomed a black dorsal fin as high as she was long. Wobbling slightly from side to side, the great fin moved directly toward her. Feeling the whale's sound beam wash over her belly like a stream of tiny bubbles, she knew that she had been detected. She flipped over backwards and streaked toward shore.

The young female had traveled scarcely a quarter-mile, when she found herself plunging into the midst of a dozen mackerel sharks of the species commonly known as porbeagles. Probably attracted by the explosions, perhaps also following the scent of blood and oil from the slaughtered bluefins, the porbeagles circled the dolphin somewhat warily. They were sizable sharks, six feet long on average, with a few in the group ranging the better part of eight feet in length.

As the young dolphin darted this way and that, seeking a safe route out of the shark school, the porbeagles became increasingly excited and started mobbing her. One of them butted her with its snout, something sharks often do just prior to taking a first bite. She was in grave danger.

Terrified, she sounded her distress whistle and soared high above the surface, taking air as she hurdled over the massed sharks. The splash of her re-entry further excited the porbeagles, and they pursued her.

Through instinct or a dawning shrewdness, driven by sheer fright, the young female leaped along the surface, changing direction each time she re-entered the water. Confused by the dolphin's zigzag course, the sharks fell behind, but continued their pursuit in her general direction. Fatigue returned. The dolphin's leaps became progressively shorter, the distance between her and the sharks progressively smaller.

Suddenly, several large black and white shapes flashed by on either side of her. Moments later, she heard a series of heavy thuds. Glancing back the next time she cleared the surface, she saw a shark hurled twenty feet out of the water by an orca's flukes. Another orca breached, crushing a large porbeagle in its jaws as it leaped. A third orca seemed to be circling the others, as though keeping the sharks contained.

The exhausted young dolphin continued slowly on, frightened by the carnage behind her. The earlier reactions of her mother and nanny had suggested that orcas were to be feared, yet it appeared that orcas had saved her from almost certain death.

The reason for the orcas' action was nearby, so close, in fact, that the confused white-side nearly blundered into it. An orca mother and calf, escorted by two adults, were floating at the surface two hundred yards from the area where the porbeagles were under attack. Still so frightened and short of breath that she could make only weak and intermittent use of her sonar, the young dolphin approached within twenty yards before she sensed the whales' presence.

Startled, she swung back and to the left, only to find all escape routes cut off as the whales who had attacked the sharks closed in from the west. Too winded to dive, so terrified that she was nearly in shock, she circled slowly at the surface and sounded her distress whistle.

The orca calf swam toward her. As she evaded him, the orcas nearest her gave way, as though allowing her more space in which to maneuver. There was much vocalization among the adult orcas. Now one of the big males urged the calf on by nudging it with his head. With a burst of speed the calf reached the young dolphin and grasped her flukes in his jaws, but she escaped without injury, for though the calf was twice her size, he was toothless. Around and around the ominous game continued, bounded by the adults, who extended their formation when the dolphin needed more swimming room, but kept her always contained.

Sensing that the orca calf could not do extensive damage, short of ramming her, the young dolphin concentrated on regaining her strength. Able to elude the calf with fair ease because of her smaller size and his ineptitude, she conserved her energy and watched for an opportunity to escape the adults' formation. Bit by bit, she extended her evasive maneuvers until the adult orcas were leaving large gaps in their ranks when they moved out of her way. Meanwhile, she continued to sound her distress call and listen for signs of her herd.

141

The bombs had long since stopped exploding, but the only calls audible to her seemed to be orca cries coming from all directions.

The young white-side's breathing had returned to normal. Her muscles once again felt strong. She felt ready to attempt escape as soon as an opportunity presented itself, but her hopes were crushed by the appearance of another orca pod. The second pod was larger than the first, about twelve whales in all, including two young calves. Immediately, the orca sucklings were pushed into the moving arena by their adult guardians, and the young dolphin found herself being pursued by three tormentors.

As the three orca calves vied with each other, the game became more dangerous. In an effort to escape, the young dolphin went deep. This proved to be a mistake. Mobbing the dolphin, tugging at her flippers and flukes, the orca calves held her underwater until she was on the verge of drowning. Just as she was about to lose consciousness, the adults interceded and allowed her to surface for air.

The dolphin felt burning pain in her right flipper. Glancing back, she saw that it was badly scratched and bleeding. Apparently one of the calves, older than the others, had begun to sprout teeth.

The young white-side understood now what was happening. The adult orcas were using her to teach their calves how to kill.[2] And after the calves tired of their game, what then? The adults would probably tear her into pieces and feed her to the calves, as they did the bluefin tuna. The thought brought on convulsions of fear, and she retched, but there was nothing in her stomach to regurgitate. Desperately frightened and hungry, she longed for the comforting presence of her mother and nanny, yearned for a bellyful of warm milk.

Again, the orca calves rushed her, and the macabre game went on until the young dolphin was exhausted past caring. She floated at the surface, refusing to move as the calves mauled and butted her. Certain that death was inevitable, she even snapped at the calves and butted them in turn. Surprised by her sudden aggressiveness, they backed away.

The dolphin was awaiting the next onslaught when the whine of propellers turned the orcas' attention to the north. A hundred-foot vessel came into view, steaming at full speed directly toward the whales. The females moved in and collected their calves, the others formed a protective ring around them, and the combined pods moved off at a brisk pace toward the south. The vessel followed, and the young dolphin found herself alone, bobbing in the boat's wake.

The propeller noise gave way to another, long-awaited sound, the clicks and whistles of a white-side herd. It sounded far too large to be her herd, but she issued her distress call anyway. Again and again she whistled. The calls of the herd grew louder; then minutes later she was surrounded by her herd, which had apparently joined another white-side herd of sixty or more animals. Still weak from her ordeal, she snuggled between mother and nanny and rode their pressure fields as the herd moved north.

Eight

FOR THE NEXT SEVERAL DAYS, the combined herds continued northeasterly along the coast, hunting as they went. The young female noted that the farther north they proceeded the more their hunts seemed to be concentrated on herring. This was because, during the warmer months, the common sea herring gather by the billions to spawn along the coast of Maine, especially in and around Passamaquoddy Bay.

Three days into their journey north, the dolphins were joined by another herd. A fourth herd joined them the next day, and that night still another merged into the group, which now numbered nearly four hundred dolphins. By banding together, they would be better able to contain the herring schools, which made good use of the labyrinthine waterways so characteristic of the Maine coast.

With so many others their age to join them in play, it was an exciting time for the nursing calves, but their elders left them little time for frolic. The adults seemed bent on feeding themselves to bursting several times a day, and for good reason. It was early September, and already there had been two nights when the dolphins' breath smoked against the colder air. Soon the sea would start cooling down, and they would need thick coats of blubber to keep them warm.

The flow of milk from the lactating females approached flood stage as their bodies endeavored to meet the demands of their rapidly growing calves. The babies were also encouraged to feed on sardine herring, for the littlest dolphins would be most susceptible to hypothermia when the sea cooled.

On a cool, foggy morning, the dolphins reached Grand Manan Channel. All around them rose the blows of finback whales, humpbacks, minkes, and pilot whales. Also present were white-beaked dolphins, harbor porpoises, harbor seals, and many large groups of white-sided dolphins, some numbering a thousand or more animals. All were there for the same reason, to hunt the hordes of autumn-spawning herring.

The area around Grand Manan Island teemed with herring, but was also thick with fishing vessels and hazardous nets. The herd turned northerly toward West Quoddy Head.

The herring again became enormously abundant as the dolphins approached shore, but the great schools clustered around the many small islands, finding safety in water too shallow for the dolphins. The herd leaders made no attempt to pursue the herring into the shoals, but continued on, past West Quoddy Head and into the Quoddy Narrows.

Keeping to the channel, the dolphins made their

way through Lubec Narrows, going deep when they encountered vessels. The young female was a bit edgy when she saw points of land so close that she had to roll slightly to look up at the houses and trees. It reminded her of the beach where she had become lost. Also, the many recurring echoes in the narrow channel confused her, for she was accustomed to the low reverberation levels of open sea.

On and on the herd swam, northwest into Cobscook Bay, then westerly across the bay into another series of narrows. Apparently the herd leaders had been here before and had a certain destination in mind.

As the herd wended its way through swift narrows of cold, dark water, the young female saw thickly forested islands and points materialize out of the fog. On the shore she saw herons, bald eagles, and fish crows—birds that were new to her. The familiar gulls and terns were also present in astounding numbers. From below her came a din of snapping and popping sounds that suggested the bottom was swarming with lobsters, crabs, and mollusks.

The herd stopped, and the leaders milled about, clicking and whistling among themselves as though something were blocking their way. The young female reared back at the surface to take a look. She could not believe her eyes. A quarter-mile ahead, the water rose like a ten-foot-high wall. Her first view of a cataract. As though this were not enough, she heard heavy blows and saw three finback whales surface less than fifty yards to her right. Narrow quarters for dolphins, but narrower still for finback whales.

The finbacks, all fully-grown adults by the look of

them, circled quite close to the dolphins. They appeared to be lunge-feeding without relaxing their throat pouches, perhaps because they were pursuing herring and could not afford to be slowed down by drag. The great whales seemed larger than ever here in this swirling pocket of water less than a mile long and half a mile wide.

The dolphin herd leaders had either taken a wrong turn or misjudged tidal conditions, for ahead of them loomed Cobscook Falls, a cataract that reverses its direction with the swing of the tide. At present, the tide was on the ebb, flowing against the dolphins, and the falls were eight to ten feet high.

The dolphins cast about the small bay in search of food, but the pickings proved lean. The whales had already caught or frightened away most of the herring.[1] The herd leaders swung south around Falls Island, taking the longer route into Dennys Bay.

As soon as the dolphins rounded Falls Island, they heard the faint bladder squeaks of herring in the bay about a mile northwest of them. Clearing the narrow channel, the herd spread out across Dennys Bay, making a great sweep between Hallowell Island and Dram Island. Clearly audible now were the bladder squeaks from hordes of frightened brit, young herring just above sardine size.

The only escape route for the young herring was into the shallow brackish waters of Dennys River and Hardscrabble River. Perhaps the dolphins knew that herring dislike brackish water and would instead seek refuge in the area's many small coves. That would enable the dolphins to feed at their leisure on the trapped fish. Apparently, this is why the herd leaders had ventured into such dangerous waters so far from the open sea. They must have hunted here before, and with great success.

Sure enough, the massive shoal of brit approached the river mouths, then divided like a fountain and doubled back on either side of the dolphins, pouring into the various coves in such vast numbers that the water writhed with their passage. The vanguard of each school reached safety in shallow water, but the dolphins wreaked havoc on the rest.

The sun was low, the tide well on the ebb. The young female, her mother, and her nanny were working Lingley Cove near Hallowell Island. Suddenly, disaster. Cries of distress filled the cove. The herd leaders had misjudged the speed of the area's twenty-foot tides. Many dolphins were being stranded on the rapidly shoaling mud flats in Lingley Cove, and as many more again, trying to help their comrades, were themselves becoming trapped. Whistling and squealing in terror, they struggled desperately to free themselves, but their thrashing merely stirred the banks into a quagmire. Some sank so deeply into the soft mud that they suffocated immediately. The rest lay mired far from water now as the tide quickly emptied the cove.

Nor had the tragedy yet run its course. Because of their smaller size, some babies had swum clear of the mud, only to find they had left their mothers behind. Desperate to reach their mothers, the babies hurled themselves onto the mud banks. Some free-swimming adults managed to grasp the flukes of a few youngsters

148

and pull them free, but the babies merely stranded themselves again. Over a hundred and fifty dolphins lay trapped in the mud. The rest circled frantically outside the cove, answering the calls of the stranded. Their piteous cries filled the gathering twilight.

An engine roared on a nearby road. The dolphins heard the double slam of doors, then a series of sharp explosions. Small objects, moving too fast for the eye to see, began spattering the mud and thudding into the bodies of the helpless animals on the strand.

A pickup truck appeared on the road overlooking the cove. Two young men with rifles got out of the truck and began firing at the helpless dolphins. The light was failing fast, but they manage to score a few hits before darkness settled over the cove. Laughing, they climbed back into their truck and roared off down the road.

Responding to a telephoned complaint of rifle shots being fired near a residence, Inland Warden Ernest Smith arrived at Lingley Cove about eight-thirty that evening, in time to apprehend two persons who were attempting to drag one of the dolphins ashore and butcher it. Having dealt with the offenders, Smith assessed the situation on the strand by lanternlight, then summoned help from the marine biology station in nearby Edmunds.

Now separated from their stranded comrades by a considerable expanse of mud, the dolphins saw lights bobbing in the cove. Several men were making their way onto the mud flats. One of the men sank nearly to his chest in ooze and had to be rescued by the others.

Rearing back in the slack water just outside the cove, the free dolphins watched anxiously as the men moved among the stranded ones, shining their lights on the animals and squatting down to examine them. The men moved farther out on the mud flats, then hauled two sucklings over the mud and into the water. Still crying out to their stranded mothers, the babies waited until the men left the water, then hurled themselves back onto the mud flats. The men refloated the young dolphins, only to have them once again strand themselves. The situation seemed hopeless, but the men refloated the dolphins for a third time, then shouted and clapped their hands to drive them into deeper water.

Sensing that the men were trying to help, the free dolphins moved closer to the strand. As they did, they found the water littered with dead and dying herring that had been regurgitated by the stranded dolphins. When the men for the third time refloated two babies and frightened them away from the strand, six adult dolphins sprinted into the shallows and herded the youngsters into deeper water, where they were contained by the others.

The men faced a formidable task, for the water had retreated steadily farther from the strand, making it necessary to carry the slippery, frantically struggling babies over considerable distances through deep mud. Nonetheless, they managed to haul two more babies off the strand and drive them into deeper water. Unseen by the men, adult dolphins quickly pressed in on both sides of the sucklings and bore them away to the waiting herd, where they were restrained and comforted by the females.

Throughout the evening, the men bent to the arduous task, carrying the smallest babies and dragging larger animals across the mud and into the water. During all that time, the remnants of the various herds circled nearby in Dennys Bay, containing freed babies and supporting older animals too weakened by stress to swim on their own.

Toward midnight, a new danger threatened the dolphins still trapped in the mud. The tide was returning. In a few hours the cove would be flooded again, and any animals still mired in mud would surely drown.

As the water moved steadily closer to the strand, the men began using outboard motorboats and ropes to haul dolphins out of the mud. In a desperate race against time and tide, they freed many animals but again most of them restranded themselves. Then black water swirled over the strand, and the frightened cries of the doomed animals took on renewed urgency. Their calls were answered by the herd in the bay. For a time, the stranded animals continued to cry out and then, one by one, fell silent as the advancing waters extinguished their final sparks of life. Despite the valiant efforts of the men, only about twenty dolphins were freed. One-hundred-thirty-seven dolphins lay dead in the mud.[2]

The night of tragedy and pain gave way to a bright, unseasonably warm day. Most of the orphaned babies had been distracted from their losses by lactating females, who allowed them to share milk with their own offspring, but a few still showed signs of bolting for the strand unless they were continually restrained.

During the night, while the tide was at flood stage, a few scouts had entered the cove to search for signs of life. They had returned, silent and subdued. Not a sound had been heard from the stranded animals since the return tide covered them, yet the herd lingered in the bay, hoping that more of their comrades would somehow be returned to them.

Time passed like a sluggish current, but finally, the tide was once again on the ebb. Slowly, the cove gave up its waters, but not its dead. Throughout that long, hot day, the dolphins circled in the bay, watching the final fate of their comrades unfold. [3]

Outboard motorboats, nine in all, converged on the cove. Men attached lines to the tails of the dead and towed the corpses into the shallows beneath the high bluff, where a pulp-loader stood, its cable hanging down into the water. One by one, the handsomely striped bodies were hoisted out of the water and loaded onto a refrigerated truck. All day and well into the night, scientists and local people labored, salvaging as many corpses as they could extricate from the tight grip of the mud. The final tally: 62 specimens. The other corpses were so deeply mired that the men could not remove them.

The dolphins' loss was the scientists' gain. Never before had so many fresh specimens of *Lagenorhynchus acutus* been made available for postmortem studies.

152

Fifty-nine specimens were trucked to the New England Aquarium in Boston. The other three went to a Canadian research facility. In Boston, the bodies were frozen and later autopsied by a team of researchers funded by the U.S. Marine Mammal Commission. The final report filled 160 pages. Combining the data from this investigation with those gathered after earlier strandings, scientists also published conclusions as to herd composition, birthing seasons, gestation and lactation periods, postnatal growth, maturation ages, life expectancy, and food preferences.[4]

Except for a few local newspaper accounts, this tragedy received little public attention.

The young female, her mother, and her nanny escaped injury, but their original herd suffered many casualties. Four mothers, two babies, and four yearlings were lost, together with one old male and two elderly females. The three elders were the most experienced members of the herd, so their loss would be felt for some time to come. Then again, the survivors might be better off without them, for the elders were responsible for leading the others into those dangerous waters. Perhaps they had become lazy with age and had chosen easy feeding in a bottleneck like Dennys Bay despite the danger. Whatever the reasons for venturing so far inland, many paid with their lives.

Nor had the survivors necessarily left all the dying behind them. Even now, as the combined herds retraced their route back to the Bay of Fundy, six of their number had to be pushed along at the surface, for they were so weakened by stress that they could scarcely swim. The others rescued by the men were strong enough to swim on their own, but seven of these were orphaned sucklings, whereas only six females lost their babies. Each of these may adopt a baby, once they get over the shock of the stranding, but what of the other orphan? The unstressed nursing females had been allowing the orphans to share their milk, but if they continued doing so, their own offspring might suffer from malnutrition. No, the dying was not necessarily over, by any means.

Clearing Quoddy Narrows, the dolphins proceeded due south across the Bay of Fundy. The pace was slow, limited by the continuing need to support six stress-weakened dolphins at the surface. Another day passed before the herd left Cape Sable, Nova Scotia, behind and moved on into open sea.

Under normal circumstances, the temporary amalgamation of herds would probably have redivided by now, but the common bonds of suffering and need kept the animals together. Whenever prey was detected, about half the dolphins broke away to hunt, then returned to care for the helpless ones while the other half of the herd took its turn at feeding.

By noon of the following day, four of the stressed animals were swimming on their own, but the other two had slipped into coma. That night, one of them stopped breathing altogether. Shortly after sunrise, the other comatose animal's vital signs flickered and faded. The dolphins continued to bear the lifeless bodies along with them for another day and night. Then they gave the corpses a final nuzzling examination and released them to the deep.

As the young female watched the corpses sink out of sight, she was still trying to grasp what happened in the cove. Many far wiser than she felt just as confused. Even now, days after the stranding, all were stunned by the loss. Herd leadership seemed vague, ever shifting, and social vocalization was minimal.

She was not certain how many from her original herd had been lost, but many familiar voices were missing. She especially felt the absence of two of her age who had become close companions. While all surviving sucklings from her original herd still had their mothers, two females had lost their babies, and their voices were still charged with stress.

The orphans tried repeatedly to get milk from the females who had lost their babies, but stress seemed to have interrupted their lactation, so the orphans nursed along with the sucklings who still had mothers. Already, the young female could feel the effects of sharing her milk with others. Each feeding being smaller than usual, hunger drove her back to the mammary slit that much sooner, but there never seemed to be enough milk. Her mother had begun pushing the orphans away, but their cries were terrible to hear.

Wandering easterly over Browns Bank, the dolphins encountered a pod of several hundred pilot whales. They joined the whales to hunt squid along the northern periphery of Browns Bank.

The next day, death again struck the white-sides. Two of the orphaned sucklings, perhaps weakened by malnutrition, fell behind the herd during a high-speed hunt and were attacked by a school of porbeagles. By the time the adults heard the babies' cries and circled back to help, the sharks had torn them to pieces.

Good fortune soon followed bad, though. Over the next week or so, lactation resumed in six females who had survived the stranding but lost their babies. They soon adopted the five remaining orphans, and herd life settled into a semblance of normalcy.

There is no evidence of dolphins adopting orphaned babies in the wild. In fact, scientists reporting on the Lingley Cove stranding expressed doubt that any of the orphans survived.

I prefer an optimistic, albeit speculative, outcome. There is ample evidence that cetaceans go to great lengths to help each other, even to the extent of sacrificing their lives. So pervasive is this altruistic tendency that even cetaceans of different species are frequently observed helping each other. Accordingly, I doubt that the orphaned sucklings in this story would be allowed to die if there were lactating females available who had lost their own babies. The Lingley Cove stranding data do not rule out the possibility of such females being available, so I have opted for a happy note and let most of the orphans survive.

For more on the topic of care-giving behavior among cetaceans, see "Are Dolphins Reciprocal Altruists?" by Richard Connor and Kenneth Norris, in *The American Naturalist*, March 1982.

Nine

AN OVERCAST NOVEMBER NIGHT. The sea was "firing." Wisps of blue-green light trailed from the tips of the dolphins' flippers and flukes. Their faces took on an eerie glow. Phantasmal bubbles trailed from blowholes, rose to the surface, and burst like showers of colored sparks.

The young female swam on her back, releasing bubbles so that she could watch them rise and burst. The sparkle pleased her. Now she executed a snap roll and broke the surface in a soaring leap so precisely calculated that she dropped smoothly back into her original position in the steadily moving herd. Her sparkling breach stirred a flurry of excitement. Dozens of youngsters skittered along the surface on their sides and backs, raising great clouds of bioluminescent spray. Many adults joined in, leaping twenty or more feet in the air, each leap leaving a brief arch of sparkling water droplets. Some turned forward somersaults as they soared above the surface, and the spray from their spinning bodies formed fiery pinwheels. Soon the entire

157

herd of nearly three hundred dolphins was engaged in exuberant play.

A loud danger crack from an elder brought play to an abrupt halt. Six leaders spread out, facing north. They listened for a time, then turned back and circled at a leisurely pace, their heartbeats normal. Play resumed.

The young female heard a brief trumpeting call, like the sound made by a humpback pinching its nostrils slightly as it blows. Now she saw bushy showers of bioluminescence rising above the calm sea. Six or more humpbacks were heading south. All the humpbacks she encountered lately seemed to be heading south, usually in groups of three or more.

As the whales approached, the dolphins continued their exuberant leaps, turning the sea and the air above it into a great light display. The humpbacks swung left and circled the dolphins. One of them lob-tailed the surface, then swam on its back with both flippers pointed skyward. For the young white-side female, the sight triggered fond remembrances of the gentle humpback with the stick-shaped mark on his flukes.

She disengaged herself from the herd and swam toward the whale, making squealing blowhole sounds as she approached. The humpback rolled over and sounded a trumpet blow. It was too dark to see his flukes, but she felt certain this was the same whale. She swam on her back, waggling her flippers, and the whale did the same. Now the whale submerged with the tips of his long white flippers cutting the surface, and she swam between them, darting from one flipper to the other and flicking her flukes against him as she turned.

When she tired of that game, she settled against the humpback's belly and let herself be carried along by his pressure field. Suddenly, the whale sounded a trumpeting call so powerful it frightened her. Her head ringing from the intense sound, she flipped to the surface.

Another humpback approached from behind her. She turned and pointed her beak in its direction, scanning the whale with clicks, then listening in the passive mode. Why, this whale had two heartbeats. One lub-a-dubbed slowly, like a normal whale's heart; the other was faster and not as loud. She scanned the humpback with ultrasound and acoustically perceived a baby, as long as two adult dolphins, moving inside the female's womb. Was she about to witness the birth of a whale?

Already fifteen feet long, the humpback fetus seemed due for delivery, but another month or more would pass before the mother reached full term. By then she would be in tropical waters, where her baby would have a few months to grow strong and fat before returning with its mother to the cold-water feeding grounds.

The pregnant humpback glided past the young dolphin, gently grazed the male with her flipper, and continued south with the other four whales that made up their migration group. The male, who had been floating belly up, rolled over with a great slap-slap of flippers against the surface, then set off after the others with such a surge of fluke power that the young dolphin was swept away as though on a river current.

When the friendly humpback had gone, the young female returned to the herd, which had settled into a slowly turning sleep circle. As she made her way beneath the others, seeking her mother and nanny, she noticed for the first time that quite a few white-side females had double heartbeats, too. The babies sounded tiny, though, for they had been conceived only four or five months earlier and would not be born until the following spring or summer.

Recognizing, from among the hundreds of other calls, the periodic whistles of her mother and nanny, she swam over and slipped between them. They roused long enough to greet her with nuzzling caresses, then resumed their moving naps. The overcast cleared, and a full moon swam through high, filmy clouds.

She was too preoccupied to sleep. So many humpbacks were heading south, hardly ever stopping to feed or play. Petrels, shearwaters, and many other seabirds also seemed to be flying south lately.

A great chevron of geese passed overhead, outlined against the moonglow, pulsing with honking calls that ranged the length and breadth of the formation, much the way whistle-calls of dolphins move throughout a herd. The little dolphin was conscious of the seasonal change, a time of flight for many creatures. Would the dolphin herd soon head south as well? Instead, it seemed to her, they moved farther easterly every day. Bottom echoes were long returning now.

She heard wispy pulses of sound below her and saw many faintly glowing shapes darting about in the depths. A school of squid jetting along at high speed. Pursuing or being pursued? Why did the adults not awake and go after them? Short-finned squid seemed to be their favorite food. She favored them, too, now that her teeth could grip their slimy skin long enough for her to swallow. They had a sour oily flavor and a rubbery squirm when they struggled between her jaws. After a night squid hunt, each dolphin countenance was smeared with iridescent slime and glowed brightly in the darkness. She liked that, after a squid hunt.

Mother's milk was still her chief food, though. She did not have to chase it, and it did not bite back.

So many double heartbeats. Soon there would be more babies to take the place of those who died in the mud. Never again would she go where the ocean bottom rose into the air, even if the elders wished it. There lay danger, and puzzlement, for some humans seemed intent on harming dolphins while others helped them. There seemed to be different kinds of humans, some like dolphins and others like sharks, but she could not distinguish one from the other.

Something was blocking out the sounds from bottom creatures directly below her. A massive zone of silence seemed to be passing below her. She pointed her beak downward and emitted a burst of clicks that brought the entire herd awake with a start. Her echoes returned, quick and hard. The thing was about midway between her and the bottom, and it was enormous, many times larger than the biggest whale she had ever heard. She heard a whirring sound, then the faint swish of a propeller. A submarine the size of eight finback whales! The thing moved on, and in its wake, the sounds of bottom creatures returned.

The adults settled back into their naps as though nothing unusual had happened, but the young female was more wide awake than ever. It was her first encounter with a submarine, and her brain recorded equal parts fascination and fear.

She dropped back a bit and swung under her mother to nurse for a while. The warm milk relaxed her, and she was soon napping with the rest.

Daybreak found the herd in continental slope waters over the great Northeast Channel, halfway between Browns Bank and Georges Bank. The water was warm enough for the smallest sucklings, but the air was cold. Each breath left a burning sensation in the young female's blowhole.

Something was happening among the adults, something she did not understand. They were milling about, clicking and whistling as though trying to reach a decision. This continued for some time; then part of the herd separated, sorted out its leadership, and swam southwesterly. The young female's maternal herd remained with the larger group, which headed northeasterly.

They would winter, as had generations of their kind before them, in the more northerly reaches of the continental slope waters. The other dolphins, themselves following customs many generations old, would winter far to the south in the New York Bight.

Perhaps, come the following spring, they would all meet again in the Gulf of Maine.

The days were growing shorter and colder. Even at midday, now, the sun seemed halfway toward its setting, and each time the dolphins surfaced, their breath left puffs of vapor suspended above the waves. The water was comfortable, though, for they stayed well within the warming precincts of the Gulf Stream.

Throughout November and December, the dolphins encountered southbound groups of humpback whales. The migration progressed in three waves. First came the gravid females, usually escorted by resting females, mothers with their yearling calves, and an occasional old male. Next to turn south were the sexually prime males, who followed a few weeks behind the mature females. Now meandering south were the juveniles of both sexes, who often paused to feed and play, for they were not urged on by the thump of fetal flukes or the pressure of swelling gonads.

While many humpbacks spend the summer in the Gulf of Maine, thousands of others summer as far north as Greenland and Iceland. Each winter, they all migrate to tropical waters, and for several months subsist on food reserves stored in their blubber. While gravid females bear and nurse their babies, males sing, breach a great deal, and mate with available females. When the suckling calves are fit to travel, the northward migration resumes, and come spring, the whales reappear on their feeding grounds.

Two intriguing mysteries surround the migratory habits of these animals. For one thing, while en route, they leave scarcely a trace on the scientific records. It is as though, between their temperate feeding grounds and their tropical calving/mating grounds, they drop out of sight. Also, one major group prefers to winter in warm shoal waters off the northwest coast of Africa,

163

while another favors the waters between Bermuda and the Caribbean basin. Despite the great distances between them, and their habit of changing songs each year, humpback males wintering off the west coast of Africa sing the same song as those wintering near the West Indies. With thousands of miles separating the two populations of whales, it seems highly unlikely that they can hear each other, yet they somehow agree on each mating season's "hit tune." They may, while southbound, experiment with new songs and arrive at a musical consensus before going their separate ways. If that were the case, though, at least one research vessel should by now have heard southbound humpbacks singing, for though their migration routes may be a mystery, sensitive equipment can detect their songs from many miles away. As of this writing, no enroute singing has been reported.

Early morning over the continental slope. The whitesides encountered a hundred or more pilot whales that appeared to be hunting, and joined them. Many of the female pilot whales had suckling calves swimming at their flanks.

Ten spotted dolphins flashed across the line of hunt, then suddenly thrust themselves out of the water and tail-walked in a tight circle, their beaks pointing skyward. They maintained their circular formation for a few seconds, then dropped back into the water. Moments later, they again rose out of the sea in a nearly perfect circle, so close together that their flippers were touching. Six times they performed this strange maneuver, then swam out of sight.[1]

All that morning the white-sides stayed with the pilot whales. Knowing that potheads feed mainly on squid, the dolphins may have deduced that they would improve their chances of finding and containing large squid schools if they hunted with the whales. Thus far, though, not a single squid had been detected.

About midday, whispers of pulsed sound were heard far below. The dolphins and pilot whales went deep. As the young female swam between her mother and nanny, she felt the increasing pressure squeeze her rib cage. At a depth of six hundred feet, the hunters leveled off. The squid were audible above them now. Pilot whales in the center, dolphins on either side, the cetaceans fanned out and ascended in silence, homing in on the faint sounds made by the squids' water-ejecting nozzles.

Approaching from below, their black backs camouflaged against the dark depths, the cetaceans are doubtless invisible to the sharp-eyed cephalopods. In such situations, stealth is apparently advisable, for squid can jet off at speeds even the swiftest dolphins find difficult to match.

The hunters had fared well. Silhouetted against the distant surface glow was a large school of short-finned squid, which suddenly darted toward the surface, rising two hundred feet in a few seconds. At first, the young female thought her hunting party had been detected, but then she remembered that squid usually eject ink decoys when pursued, and she saw no signs that these squid had done so.

The whales and dolphins followed and found the squid attacking a school of six-inch mackerel fry. Applying the same hunting techniques that the dolphins used, the main body of the squid school surrounded and contained the mackerel, while small groups took turns darting in to feed. Each squid seized a fish with its tentacles and delivered a killing bite to the nape of the neck. Then, holding the fish in its tentacles, the squid quickly reduced it to a skeleton. Those who had fed dropped back into the school, and others moved in to get their share.

While the squid were preoccupied with their own hunt, the pilot whales and dolphins struck. Their first pass was silent and productive, but then the squid ejected ink decoys and scattered, and the cetaceans had to start echo-clicking in order to follow them. The squid regrouped into several smaller schools and jetted off in various directions, hoping to confuse and divide their pursuers, but the cetaceans maintained their formation and pursued the largest school.

The hunt moved closer to the surface, where the young female could see clearly for several body lengths. The squid seemed far too swift for the pilot whales, but the potheads were somehow managing to catch their share. Observing one of them closely, she learned why. Instead of simply clicking to echolocate the squid, the pilot whales were emitting sharply focused pulses of sound so intense that they stunned the squid long enough for the whales to catch them. The adult dolphins, too, were emitting single pulses of gunshot intensity. Although these were not powerful enough to stun the large squid, they made them swerve, enabling the dolphins to cut individuals out of the school. The adult dolphins worked cooperatively in pairs and threes, using their pulses to direct squid into each other's jaws.

A foot or more in length, these squid were too large for the young female's gullet, but she experimented with the adults' pulsing technique and found that she could indeed make squid change direction.

Seeing a school of mackerel fry dart to the left as the noisy hunt swept past, she swung away from the others long enough to test her pulsations on the young fish. To her delight, she was able to stun a few mackerel. She swallowed them and hurried to catch up with the herd.

While still a bit removed from the din of the hunt, she heard heavy creaking sounds and, looking back, saw several large shapes churning the surface a hundred yards behind her. Flickering shafts of sunlight slanted into the depths, silhouetting the creatures and obscuring details, but the sight stirred memories of six months ago, when she had seen the silvery gray undersides of sperm whales pass dangerously close overhead.

The pilot whales and dolphins quickly abandoned their hunt and branched off to the left and right, just as the large creatures dove and headed their way. The young female and her guardians happened to be at the rear of the white-side herd, and were among the last to leave the hunt line. The slow creaking noises increased in pitch to a growl, probing the young female's skin with drumming fingers of sound. Now a cannonlike pulse of sound struck her body, driving splinters of pain into her sensitive hearing canals. Again and again, the intense sound pulses struck her. She became nauseated and lost her mackerel snack.

Two adult sperm whales and a half-grown juvenile swept past, showing no interest in the fleeing pilot whales and dolphins. Ahead of the whales, the water was littered with hundreds of slowly sinking squid, which had been stunned by the whales' sound pulses. The sperm whales scooped the squid into their mouths, then continued on, alternately clicking to locate the remaining squid and emitting thunderclaps of sound to stun them.

When they were safely clear of the sperm whales, the dolphins and pilot whales regrouped and began searching for other food. Distant stun pulses, reverberating between bottom and surface like multiple hammer blows, suggested that the sperm whales were still finding prey. They may have caught up with the rest of the squid pursued earlier by the dolphins and pilot whales, but this was unlikely. All squid for miles around had probably gone to the bottom. The cephalopods are aware enough to recognize the sounds of sperm whales and take evasive action.

The young female white-side soon shook off the nauseous effects of her sonic pounding, but developed a persistent headache.

So this was how the larger, slower, toothed whales caught swift prey such as squid. She had noticed from time to time that some of the adult white-sides seemed able to disorient individual members of fish schools, but she had not associated that with the particularly loud pulsations of sound made by certain adults.

She had learned two important alternative uses of her echolocation apparatus: the stunning of small prey, and the acoustic manipulation of larger prey. She had also learned another important lesson: Never again be caught in the path of approaching sperm whales.

Eyes closed, she used "facial vision" to keep herself positioned between the flanks of her mother and nanny, and she relaxed the muscles in her head and neck until the headache dissipated.

Now nearly seven months old and six feet long, the handsome young female seemed strong and self-sufficient, yet she still relied on her mother's milk for most of her nourishment. She would continue nursing to some degree until she was about eighteen months old, perhaps even until her mother approached term with her next baby, for there was much the young dolphin had to learn if she was to survive and perpetuate the species with her own offspring.

She had been a quick learner. Already, her echolocation skills were such that she could recognize the most common forms of marine life long before they came into view. Except for certain closely related species, the various creatures yielded echoes that sounded different. The differences were often subtle, but she and her kind were equipped by nature to detect minute variations in frequency and phase relationships.

As her brain reached critical mass and her vocabulary of acoustic images approached critical volume, she began to gain her first inklings of how the adults communicated with each other.

169

Whenever they sensed something strange ahead, the leaders sounded sharp slash-call whistles of descending pitch. Everyone stopped and listened for signs of danger. The leaders ventured cautiously ahead, scanning the thing from a safe distance. The others followed close behind. If the leaders stopped and blooped large bubbles from their blowholes, it meant that they were puzzled.

Somehow—the young female had yet to determine how the choice was made—a scout volunteered or was selected to make a closer investigation. The scout swam out of sight. Clicking was heard in the distance, then the scout returned.

Much was evident from body signs. The scout's heart might beat faster than normal, say, while his or her voice lacked the sharp peaks indicative of fear. This told the young female that the scout was excited or concerned, but not afraid. The scout's posture was significant, too, and at night, was determined by touch or sonar. A head-down position suggested readiness to attack or defend. If the head was higher than the tail, however, threat was not imminent.

There was more to the adults' communication than body language, though. The young female heard them exchange complex click-bursts, whose amplitude and phase were modulated like the echoes she heard from certain objects.

One day some weeks past, a scout had returned from reconnoitering an unknown object up ahead. He then swam back and forth in front of the herd, emitting a uniform pattern of soft clicks. The sound reminded her of echoes heard when she scanned fishing nets strung between widely spaced anchor buoys. When the herd continued on, she passed close enough to the object to echo-scan it, and heard a uniform pattern of soft clicks much like the scout's. Moving closer, she saw a net in which hundreds of fish were trapped by their gill covers. Farther on, she saw a dead brown shark larger than she, tangled in the net.

The association of nets with danger and death had come easily to her. She would not forget the similarity between the scout's phonations and the sounds she heard when she echo-scanned the net, nor would she forget the sight of the trapped fish and the dead shark. Lately, she had been hearing many clicked exchanges between adults that reminded her of echo patterns heard when she scanned various creatures and objects. The realization slowly dawned that the adults might be using reconstructed echo patterns to communicate with each other, but she could not be certain until her acoustic skills developed to the point where she could try it for herself.

She could now recognize and identify the individual whistle-calls used by all in the herd for omnidirectional scanning and for keeping track of each other's whereabouts, but there were also many complex click-whistle exchanges that were totally meaningless to her. Except when they were napping, the adults carried on a continuous babble of birdlike chirps, staccato squeals, and growling sounds. She mimicked the sounds, especially those made by her mother and nanny, but she had no idea what they meant.

As with everything else, understanding would come with time. For now, she needed merely to recognize the distinctive whistle-calls of those most important to her and to increase her understanding of the echoes returned by her clicks.

First light. Elongated black clouds, their undersides red, swam the horizon like bloodied whales.

Within a few hours after sunrise, the wind was keening out of the northeast. Waves began thrusting high, peaking white, and spindrift smoked the air. The dolphins porpoised effortlessly through the heavy seas, exiting from the lee side of one wave and re-entering on the windward side of the next, letting wave energy do much of the work for them. Tatters of dark cloud scudded overhead as the winds mounted to gale force. Then after a brief but intense rainfall, the weather cleared.

The days passed in easy regularity, and the young female was surprised by the warmth of the slope waters. Most of the Gulf of Maine had been colder in midsummer than the slope waters were now, because the Gulf waters are largely isolated from the warming effects of the Gulf Stream by Georges and Browns Banks.

Sometimes the herd ventured out into the Gulf Stream, where the water was a deeper blue than any sky the young female had ever seen,[2] and tropical creatures like Portuguese men-of-war drifted by on the warm current. On one such day, a moderate wind swept down out of the north, opposing the Gulf Stream and building up waves all out of proportion to the wind strength. It was like being in the steep, high seas of a gale, but without the strong winds and spray.

Except for large transoceanic freighters or tankers

that occasionally wallowed by, most of the vessels the young female saw were sleek gray warships flying the flags of different nations. Sometimes she heard a submarine humming through the perpetual darkness below her. She had yet to see one surface for air, but they sounded to her as though they were shaped more like whales than vessels. Now and then, she saw skate-shaped aircraft flash overhead, chased by their sounds, unlike anything in the sea.

Far away a fin whale moaned. A short time later, something large passed below the herd, making no sound, its presence evident only by the bottom sounds it blocked out as it passed. Thinking it a whale, the young female emitted a loud snap to determine its depth. Her "whale" scattered into bits—a school of fish. Thousands of fish moving as one, continually changing leaders. Her learning process compared the movements with those of cetaceans.

Next day the clouds were swollen black and billowing low. The wind was hushed, the sea as flat as an oil slick. Toward midmorning, plump raindrops began dimpling the smooth surface. The dolphins swam slowly, enjoying the soft bell-like beat of the rain. The young female turned on her side to let the sweet drops patter on her tongue. Water from the sky did not taste like seawater—a mild sensuous pleasure.

Soon the air temperature fell and the surface was drummed by sleet. The ice pellets stung the dolphins' heads, and the incessant roar at the surface hurt their sensitive hearing canals, so they made long, deep dives until the sleet passed.

When the surface roar stopped, the dolphins ascended and broke water to find themselves in a heavy snowfall. Those born that year were wide-eyed as fat snowflakes sank slowly seaward, swirled now and then by puffs of wind. It was as if the stars were falling. The curious dolphin caught some snow on her tongue and found that, when melted, it tasted much the same as rain. While everyone was very quiet, cruising through the snowfall, she could hear the large flakes melting into the sea with the gentlest of audible sighs. Caught up in a serenity of sight, sound, and taste, feeling secure in the herd's togetherness, she fell behind her mother and nanny.

A piercing whistle from her mother, and she hurried to catch up as the others moved, more cautiously now, through the falling whiteness. They approached what appeared to be several rocky islands, nearly awash, curiously capped by a layer of snow. A vapor cloud rose. One island rolled a bit. Three sperm whales were sleeping at the surface. The dolphins passed well clear, very quietly, and continued toward the north.

It was the end of a dolphin summer.

Afterword

DOLPHINS ARE SUCH BRIGHT, social, vocal creatures that anyone studying them is sorely tempted to credit the animals with some sort of language capability. Scientists have extensively analyzed dolphin phonations, hoping to break any code that may exist, but as far as I can determine, no one has been able to establish a correlation between a signal sent by one dolphin and a response elicited from another dolphin. In other words, it appears that scientists have been unable to interpret a single acoustic signal emitted by dolphins as having semantic content. Bastian claimed to demonstrate that arbitrary environmental information was transmitted between two captive bottlenose dolphins, but other scientists feel that his experiments have not been confirmed.[1]

According to Busnel and Classe, all correlation attempts as of 1976 had focused on the animals' whistles.[2] Apparently, no one has sought semantic content in their pulsed sounds. The re-creation of echo patterns for communication, as was suggested in the last chapter, is a possibility suggested by Bunnell and Warshall a decade ago, and it surprises me that no researchers have pursued this.[3] Perhaps I have overlooked something during my research.

Using the Freedom of Information Act, I asked the Naval Ocean Systems Center in San Diego for all findings on cetacean communications. They referred me to the *Annotated Bibliography of Publications from the U.S. Navy's Marine Mammal Program*, updated July 1, 1980. Most of the papers covered by that bibliography are quite dated. Many were already familiar to me. When I pressed for more recent findings, Captain D. B. Murton assured me that the bibliography "encompasses all records available at NOSC on the subjects of cetacean language, intelligence, and communications." Responding to my comment that the citations are quite dated, he wrote, "the Navy's Marine Mammal Program has not been involved in research on these subjects for some period of time."

Despite our inability to discover the Rosetta Stone of dolphin "language," that these animals do exchange signals has been established through numerous observations.[4] Unfortunately, their signals doubtless bear no resemblance to language, as we know it, and that is why it is such a Herculean task to decipher them. We would probably have an easier time understanding extraterrestrial technologists, because with them we should at least share the common grounds of science and mathematics.

Instead of trying to decipher the "speech" of animals (or to teach them to speak our language, as John C. Lilly attempted to do with dolphins), scientists can sometimes meet animals halfway by using artificial lan-

176

guages. Although there is much controversy on the matter, apes trained to sign do appear able to manipulate language elements at least to the level of a very young child. Bottlenose dolphins, trained in artificial whistle languages by Batteau at the China Lake Naval Ordnance Test Station, demonstrated that they could at least parallel the early human stages of verbal mimicry. (Batteau's death terminated this experiment.)[5]

University of Hawaii's Louis Herman taught two bottlenose dolphins a twelve-word sonic language and was excited by how swiftly one of them grasped simple sentences.[6] His experiments were interrupted in 1977, when two lab attendants freed the animals, charging that they were being mistreated. "Humans have no right to hold intelligent, feeling beings like dolphins in captivity," they claimed. One of the men, Kenneth LeVasseur, went so far as to say, "All these scientists are businessmen, slaveholders." Dr. Herman pressed grand theft charges and started anew with two more dolphins.

John C. Lilly's visionary work during the sixties played a major part in uplifting the public's attitude toward cetaceans. He became a popular figure, inspiring much romanticized speculation about dolphins, and this was deplored by the scientific community. Dr. Lilly has been criticized by fellow scientists for his attempts—and claimed success—at teaching English to bottlenose dolphins, for anthropomorphizing the animals, and for his experiments with LSD. Still, his contributions to our knowledge of cetaceans are legion, and his work has probably saved millions of animals by making the public aware of their intelligence and gentle sensitivity.

In 1968, Lilly terminated his dolphin work because, he said, "I no longer wanted to run a concentration camp for my friends." Within a few weeks after he stopped his research, five of the eight dolphins at his laboratory apparently took their own lives. Some starved themselves; others simply stopped breathing. Dr. Lilly freed the remaining three animals and closed his laboratory, saying he would never again experiment with dolphins unless the animals could come and go as they pleased, working with him when they wished and returning to sea when they did not.

Dr. Lilly devoted the next several years to continued isolation tank and LSD experiments, then in 1975 began another attempt to communicate with dolphins, using a computer language he called Janus. Something, perhaps financial restrictions, shattered his dream of a seaside laboratory where free dolphins could come and go as they pleased, for unless conditions have changed since this writing, his dolphins are captives.

Scientists at a number of research facilities are using visual symbols in attempts to develop artificial languages for human-dolphin communications. Results have been encouraging but limited, perhaps because the animals are by nature acoustically, not visually, oriented.

Again, all these attempts involve artificial languages of one sort or another. If we are ever to break the code of dolphin communications, we may have to come up with a sonic "template" matching system along the lines of those used in speech recognition/synthesis technology.

The process might work like this.

1. Phonations, isolated by species (and/or individuals) are recorded in all domains simultaneously; amplitude, frequency, and phase as functions of time and each other, for example.
2. The sonagrams are cross-referenced to observed behavior of sender and receiver animals.
3. The sonagrams are converted to digital form and stored on a computer disk, sectored by species and domain, and coded as to behavior.
4. The computer searches for full or partial "template" matches within and between domains and species.
5. Given acoustical matches, acoustical and behavioral matches are sought within and between domains and species.
6. Possible acoustical and behavioral matches are tested by playing the phonations back to the animals.

If standardized recording procedures were used at a number of research facilities, and if all sonagrams were fed into a central computer, recognizable patterns might emerge.

In *Whistled Languages* (p. 99), Busnel and Classe state that "physical characteristics of the [dolphin] signals appear to vary between wide limits from one individual to the next, which makes it improbable that they possess a specific semantic content."

Perhaps the signals vary widely because dolphins' "voices" differ from one to another much as ours do. By using computer-based speech recognition/synthesis technology along the lines described, we might isolate the peculiarities of "voice" and identify common patterns in phrasing.

179

The technology for storage, retrieval, and comparison of acoustic signal packets is already commercially available. Simultaneous recordings in multiple domains may not be feasible with currently available commercial instruments, but I suspect that the U.S. Navy long ago developed such equipment for underwater electronic countermeasures (ECM) and electronic warfare (EW). Perhaps an arrangement of mutual benefit could be worked out between the navy and major civilian research facilities.

It is important that we find ways to communicate with these animals. They may represent our best and certainly our least expensive near-term opportunity to make direct contact with alien intelligence. But are they any more intelligent, say, than the apes, with whom communication is relatively easy? Their brains certainly suggest that they are.

The dolphin brain poses a fascinating enigma. In terms of absolute brain size, typical dolphin species such as *L. acutus* rank above humans. Ranked by ratio of brain weight to total body weight, brain size to spinal column length, and cortical surface area to body surface area, they either match us or are a close second. Even in terms of cortical thickness, lamination, fissurization, and neuron density, the dolphin brain compares favorably with ours.

The enigma is this: Why do dolphins have such large, highly developed brains? Brainpower cannot be vital to survival in the sea, for the boned fishes and sharks have done quite nicely with minimal cephalization for hundreds of millions of years. Granted, their bodies are so superbly adapted for marine life that they can get by without large brains, but the same can be said of dolphins. Their only apparent handicap is their need to surface for air. In all other respects, they seem as well adapted as most fishes.

It has been proposed that dolphins' large, highly convoluted brains are simply sophisticated acoustic computers used for navigation and food-finding, and have nothing to do with high intelligence. This hypothesis seems weak. Bats navigate and find food acoustically with a skill rivaling that of dolphins, and yet they have primitive brains. Furthermore, why should the neocortex be the seat of intellect in our brains, yet nothing more than an acoustic computer for dolphins? Granted, the dolphin brain places its lobar emphasis on hearing, the dominant sense, but if that makes it an acoustic computer, then it seems only fair to call the human brain a visual computer. Either way, the suggestion is demeaning.

The topic of dolphin intelligence is clouded by extremism. Lay enthusiasts tend to be too anthropomorphic, while most scientists are overly anthropocentric. The white flame of scientific truth may prove visible only to open-minded researchers like Donald R. Griffin, and the truth may have nothing to do with intelligence as we define or attempt to define it. So much of our mental prowess stems from the construction of our hands that quantum mental leaps are required before we can appreciate, let alone tap, the intelligence of handless creatures such as dolphins.

This much we know: dolphins are equipped with apparently advanced brains, and they have mastered their marine environment to such a degree that they have considerable time for activities not related to survival. There must be something more than navigation, food-finding, and dreaming that keeps those large brains occupied. Nature does not squander such resources.

Perhaps we should think of the sea as a water planet that we are visiting for the first time. The dominant alien life forms are a curious and apparently bright lot. They are large and potentially dangerous, yet for the most part amazingly tolerant and gentle. Regardless of how "intelligent" they may be, there must be worthwhile lessons we can learn from such admirable creatures.

Learning, rather than teaching, may be the key that unlocks many secrets. We have learned many things about cetaceans by observing, conditioning, and dissecting them. Why not let the animals teach us for a change? They certainly show signs of wanting to do just that.

Notes and References

CHAPTER ONE

1. D. Au and D. Weihs, "At High Speeds, Dolphins Save Energy by Leaping," *Nature* 284 (5756): 548–50. Submarines designed for underwater speed are less efficient on the surface, because they lack the sharp prows needed to knife through surface tension and waves. Dolphins' bodies, too, are designed for underwater efficiency, but they must surface to breathe. When they do, they encounter surface tension and wave action. At speeds above ten knots or so, species such as *L. acutus* apparently find it more energy-efficient to leap above the surface and rid themselves of water drag while they breathe.

2. Using ultrasound, a dolphin should be able to scan the interior of another submerged creature's body, perceiving an acoustic image similar to the ultrasonic scans used in the field of medicine.

3. Cetacean babies sometimes swim to the surface as soon as their umbilical cords part. Usually, they are guided to the surface by their mothers or attendant females.

4. The reverse occurs when a cetacean begins to overheat. "An increase in blood flow near the body surface, particularly through the flippers and flukes, thermally bypasses the insulating blubber and returns the core temperature to normal." J. W. Kanwisher and S. H.

Ridgway, "The Physiological Ecology of Whales and Porpoises," *Scientific American*, June 1983, pp. 110-20.

5. At Marineland of the Pacific, Norris and Prescott saw a half-grown Pacific white-sided dolphin *(Lagenorhynchus obliguidens)* coasting alongside an adult for three complete circuits of the 80-foot tank. The smaller animal seemed always to position itself above the adult's midline with its flipper nearly or actually touching the adult's side just below the dorsal fin. Norris and Prescott observed this same "free ride" behavior on the part of the young pilot whales, orcas, common dolphins, and bottlenose dolphins.

H. R. Kelly, "A Two-Body Problem in Echelon-Formation Swimming of Porpoise," in *U.S. Naval Ordnance Test Station, China Lake, California*, 1959, Technical Note 40606-1, pp.1-7. Kelly's paper suggests that the concept of a young dolphin riding its mother's pressure field is a reasonable one, based on hydrodynamic theory.

6. Captive cetaceans are quite prone to ulcers and other stress-related disorders that greatly shorten their life spans. Orcas, for example, do well to live more than seven years in captivity, whereas their natural life expectancy may equal that of humans.

7. I did not wish to complicate matters in the text, but among cetaceans, nursing appears to be a learned behavior. The mammary slits are fairly inaccessible and must be pressed before milk will flow. The mother can help by positioning herself so that the mammary slits come in contact with the baby's mouth. However, some cetaceans born in captivity to inexperienced mothers have been unable to nurse and have had to be tube-fed by their keepers. It is thought that, in free populations, attendant females help newborn babies locate and use their mothers' mammary glands.

8. The sleep circle makes sense for the following reasons: (1) having chosen an area where there are no signs of danger within their considerable range of hearing, the animals can remain in that area by circling, thus being able to relax more than if they swam a straight course; (2) they could accomplish the same purpose by floating motionless at the surface, but this way, the animals might drift off in various directions, thereby disrupting herd integrity, (3) by circling, they retain their basic swimming forma-

tion and remain ready to make a fast and orderly escape should danger threaten.

9. Herding fish against the "wall" of the surface is one of many ways in which dolphins contain their prey. Other methods include herding prey against the bottom, against sea mounts, and against the shoreline. Some even use fish traps and gill nets as "walls" against which to herd prey.

10. John C. Lilly, *Lilly on Dolphins* (New York: Anchor/Doubleday, 1975), p. 420. Lilly observed the puncture-sealing properties of blubber in *Tursiops truncatus*. I presume that the same is true of *L. acutus*.

11. My supposition may be invalid. According to recent findings, newborn harbor porpoise *(Phocaena phocaena)* weigh as little as 20 pounds and have only a 0.4-inch thickness of blubber, yet many are born into cold inshore waters. See J. W. Kanwisher and S. H. Ridgway, "The Physiological Ecology of Whales and Porpoises," *Scientific American*, June 1983, pp. 110–20. The harbor porpoise's secret to survival, conclude Kanwisher and Ridgway, is a metabolic rate two to three times higher than that of terrestrial mammals of the same weight. The metabolic rate of *Lagenorhynchus acutus* may be as high as that of *Phocaena phocaena*, but I have yet to locate data to support this theory.

12. F. G. Wood and W. E. Evans report that a blindfolded captive dolphin repeatedly caught live fish without using echolocation; however, the animal may have been echolocating at frequencies above the response range of the observers' instruments. Also, within the confines of a quiet tank, a dolphin may be able to hear fishes' heartbeats and swimming movements. This may also be achievable at sea, but not routinely, given the typically high noise levels in the ocean.

CHAPTER TWO

1. I have no evidence of "midwifery" for *L. acutus*, but such behavior has been observed among captive cetaceans, in some cases interspecifically. For examples see David H. Brown, David K. Caldwell, and Melba C. Caldwell, "Observations on the Behavior of Wild and Captive False Killer Whales, with Notes on Associated Behavior of Other Genera of Captive Delphinids," in *Contributions in*

Science, No. 70 and 95, Natural History Museum of Los Angeles County.

2. W. N. Kellogg, *Porpoises and Sonar* (Chicago: University of Chicago Press, 1961), p. 15. Kellogg mentions cetaceans carrying dead, mutilated, or decomposing babies on their heads or backs.

Kenneth S. Norris, *The Porpoise Watcher* (New York: Norton, 1974). Norris describes a pilot whale carrying a badly decomposed baby in its mouth.

3. Lyall Watson, *The Romeo Error: A Matter of Life and Death* (New York: Anchor/Doubleday, 1974). Watson explores the problem of deciding when death actually occurs. He cites cases in which persons presumed dead "came back to life" in caskets or on autopsy tables.

4. K. S. Norris and Bertel Mohl, "Can Odontocete Cetaceans Immobilize Their Prey by Sound?" Paper presented at the Fourth Biennial Conference on the Biology of Marine Mammals, San Francisco, 1981. Norris and Mohl describe cases of seemingly unharmed prey that became immobile in the presence of dolphins and larger toothed whales. They review experiments demonstrating that fish and squid can be immobilized by sounds near those most intense for odontocetes. Notes that the latest findings for *Tursiops truncatus* (bottlenose dolphins) indicate sound power levels high enough to stun prey.

5. The bulbous foreheads of pilot whales *(Globicephala melaena)* may be comparable to those of sperm whales *(Physeter catadon)*. Both structures may have evolved for the production of sound levels intense enough to stun prey.

L. acutus is often seen with pilot whales, sometimes in groups numbering thousands of animals. As this scene suggests—and as is borne out by most harmonious interspecific activities observed in the wild—the relationship is probably symbiotic. Nonetheless, the thought that the dolphins herd fish within range of the pilot whales' stun pulses, thus conserving energy for both groups, is pure speculation on my part.

CHAPTER THREE

1. W. N. Kellogg, *Porpoises and Sonar* (Chicago: University of Chicago Press, 1961), p. 31. Kellogg suggests that porpoises (dolphins), at least while adolescent, are afraid of thunderstorms.

2. A good view of the "free ride" phenomenon is shown in archival footage used for the "Themes and Variations" segment of the BBC television series, *Life on Earth*. This has been aired by PBS affiliates in the United States.

3. Captive cetaceans are sometimes seen swimming with their flippers overlapping, as though "holding hands." This occurs in male-female pairs, as well as mother-calf pairs. Cetaceans may maintain such contact for the sake of a "free ride." Then again, it may simply show affection.

4. D. E. Sergeant; D. J. St. Aubin; and J. R. Geraci, "Life History and Northwest Atlantic Distribution of the Atlantic White-Sided Dolphin, Lagenorhynchus acutus," *Cetology* 37, September 27, 1980.

5. H. B. Bigelow and W. C. Schroeder, *Fishes of the Gulf of Maine*, Fishery Bulletin 74 (Washington, D.C.: Fish and Wildlife Service, 1953), pp. 528–31. This source cites the ocean sunfish, *Mola mola*, as a stray visitor to the Gulf of Maine, but I often see them. Their numbers may have increased since this 1953 edition, which is the latest.

6. Having witnessed firsthand the "chopping machine" ferocity of boated bluefish, and knowing of a man who lost a finger to one, I can vouch for their savage fierceness.

CHAPTER FOUR

1. "Themes and Variations" episode of BBC television series, *Life on Earth*.

2. G. Stone; S. Katona; and J. Beard, *Whales in the Gulf of Maine, 1978–1981*, Report of the Gulf of Maine Whale Sighting Network (Bar Harbor, Maine: College of the Atlantic).

3. D. Bartlett and J. Bartlett, "Patagonia's Wild Shore: Where Two Worlds Meet," *National Geographic*, March 1976, p. 315.

4. Divers marvel at the dexterity with which humpbacks maneuver their flippers and flukes to avoid injuring human observers. They are keenly aware of their reach and strength. Females sometimes gently block or push away divers who venture too close to their babies.

5. When I saw Puck turn toward the boat that day, I persuaded the skipper to shut down his engine. We were rewarded by the hour-

long visit described. I wish more skippers would turn off their engines when they encounter whales. I am convinced that, unless whales are totally preoccupied with feeding, a sudden cessation of engine noise attracts the animals. By attempting to follow whales, we disrupt their behavior and run the risk of injuring them.

6. In July 1982, the International Whaling Commission called for a complete moratorium on commercial whaling, to take effect by 1986. Japan, the Soviet Union, Norway, and Peru quickly filed formal objections. Under terms of the IWC charter, this means they can simply continue whaling. Japanese whaling companies had been thumbing their noses at IWC regulations since 1967, anyway, by acquiring whaling operations in nations that were not IWC members.

Pressure is being brought to bear on the four objecting nations, but the issue is in doubt. One major danger is that the IWC could be disbanded, leaving no international forum through which to monitor and pressure the whaling nations.

7. You can also pressure your senators and congressmen to support legislation barring the rights of whaling nations to fish in U.S. territorial waters.

CHAPTER FIVE

1. On two occasions when I observed this funnel-feeding behavior, shoals of krill were present, but whales may use this feeding method on other prey as well. It may be that the whales benefiting from this are calves being assisted by their mothers and other adults in the gathering of solid food. This could be integral to the weaning process, when the mothers encourage their babies to begin supplementing their milk diets with fish. My observations of funnel feeding occurred in August, by which time the calves are quite large (upward of thirty feet in length) and difficult to distinguish from adults, but I believe that at least some of the beneficiaries of funnel feeding were calves. Scott Mercer of New England Whale Watch, Inc., has seen humpback calves only five to six months old feeding on fish with their mothers.

Funnel feeding could also be a cooperative behavior among adults, who may take turns deflecting food such as krill into each other's mouths. They may find this method more energy-efficient than individual efforts.

2. R. W. Hult, "Another Function of Echolocation for Bottlenose Dolphins *(Tursiops truncatus),*" *Cetology,* No. 47, November 27, 1982. Hult describes captive bottlenose dolphins using high-intensity click trains to herd sea bass from one area of their tank to another and to separate individual fish from their school. The dolphins appeared to be playing with the fish. Hult quotes Kenneth Norris as saying that he and Bertel Mohl conducted experiments with spinner dolphins *(Stenella longirostris)* and found that these animals are capable of immobilizing prey with sound (see Chapter Two, note 4). Hult compares the observed captive herding behavior with herding behavior observed among *Tursiops* in the wild by these authors: D. K. Caldwell and M. C. Caldwell, *The World of the Bottlenose Dolphin* (New York: Lippincott, 1972); C. K. Taylor and G. S. Saayman, "The Social Organization and Behavior of Dolphins *(Tursiops aduncus)* and Baboons *(Papio ursinus):* Some Comparisons and Assessments," *Annals Cape Provincial Museum (Natural History),* 9 (2): 11–49; and J. Y. Cousteau, *Dolphins* (New York: Doubleday, 1975). The Cousteau book contains some questionable entries such as dolphins reaching speeds of fifty miles per hour and having more power in proportion to the weight of their muscles than any other animal. It contains many beautiful color plates of the animals, but the various species of dolphins photographed at sea are not identified.

See also V. M. Bel'kovich and A. V. Yablokov, "The Whale—An Ultrasonic Projector," *Yunyi Tekhnik (Young Technologist Magazine),* USSR, March 1963: 76–77; A. A. Berzin, *The Sperm Whale* (Jerusalem: Israel Program for Scientific Translations,); W. E. Evans, "Echolocation by Marine Delphinids and One Species of Freshwater Dolphin," *Journal of the Acoustical Society of America,* No. 54, 1973: 191–199 (Evans reports measuring a sound intensity of 70 decibels at a distance of one meter in front of the rostrum of a tank-confined *Tursiops;* energy peaks were centered in the 35- to 60-kilohertz range); and W. W. L. Au; R. W. Floyd; R. H. Penner; and A. E. Murchison, "Measurement of Echolocation Signals of the Atlantic Bottlenose Dolphin, *Tursiops truncatus* Montagu, in Open Waters," *Journal of the Acoustical Society of America,* 1974, 56 (4): 1280–90 (Sound levels of 120.4 decibels re 1 microbar were measured for one *Tursiops,* and 122.3 decibels for another; both animals were tethered in open water).

Hertz has replaced cycles per second as the international standard of frequency. Kilohertz is 1,000 hertz, or 1,000 cycles per second.

Decibel is a measurement of sound intensity, relative to the softest sound the average person can hear. Each decibel represents about a 25 percent increase in loudness above the threshold of human hearing. Ordinary conversation has about a 70-decibel intensity. A pneumatic drill of the type used to excavate streets reaches sound levels of about 100 decibels. Sound intensities of 120 decibels are a billion times louder than the softest sounds we can hear and are at our threshold of pain—that is, above 120 decibels we do not perceive the stimulus as sound per se, but feel it as pain.

3. W. E. Evans; W. W. Sutherland; and R. G. Berl, "The Directional Characteristics of Delphinid Sounds," in *Marine Bio-Acoustics*, ed. W. N. Tavolga (Elmsford, N.Y.: Pergamon Press, 1964), Vol. 1, pp. 353–72. The authors demonstrated with a *Tursiops* skull that a continuous sound source placed near the nasal sacs formed a beam directed 15 degrees above the rostrum vertically and forward horizontally. The beam pattern was very frequency-dependent in both the vertical and horizontal planes. As frequency decreased, the beam pattern broadened.

CHAPTER SIX
1. S. H. Ridgway; D. A. Carder; R. F. Green; A. S. Gaunt; and W. E. Evans, "Electromyographic and Pressure Events in the Nasolaryngeal System of Dolphins During Sound Production," in *Animal Sonar Systems*, ed. R.-G. Busnel and J. F. Fish (New York: Plenum Press, 1980), pp. 239–49. This paper strongly suggests that the overall system comprising the nasal plug nodes, diagonal membrane, and nasofrontal sacs is an excellent candidate as source and mechanism of sound production in most delphinids. The data show no evidence of sound production in the larynx.

2. T. H. Bullock and S. H. Ridgway, "Neurophysiological Findings Relevant to Echolocation in Marine Mammals," in *Animal Orientation and Navigation*, ed. S. R. Galler et al, National Aeronautics and Space Administration Publication SP-262, 1972, pp. 373–95.

3. A. E. Murchison, "Detection Range and Range Resolution of Echolocating Bottlenose Porpoise *(Tursiops truncatus),"* in *Animal So-*

nar Systems, ed. R.-G. Busnel and J. F. Fish (New York: Plenum Press, 1980), pp. 43–70.

4. K. S. Norris and W. E. Evans, "Directionality of Echolocation Clicks in the Rough-Toothed Porpoise (*Steno bredanensis* (Lesson)," in *Marine Bio-Acoustics,* Vol. 2, ed. W. N. Tavolga (Elmsford, N.Y.: Pergamon Press, 1967), pp. 305–16. Clicks of 208 kilohertz were recorded, representing some of the highest-frequency sounds ever recorded from odontocetes.

I mention that the higher pulse repetition rate (PRR) achievable by dolphins is about 1,200 pulses per second, whereas Norris and Evans cite clicks of 208 kilohertz (208,000 cycles per second). Although these statements do not conflict, they may confuse some readers. A click (pulse) is made up of many different frequencies ranging from very low to high, all bunched together in a sudden, sharp burst of sound. The sharper the pulse (in other words, the more steeply it rises and falls), the higher the frequencies it contains. Thus, the preceding reference to clicks of 208 kilohertz means that the pulses contained frequencies as high as 208,000 cycles per second, but the repetition rate at which the dolphins emitted the pulses was much lower, probably 1,200 pulses per second or less.

CHAPTER SEVEN

1. The retaliatory action taken by the tuna fishermen in my story is strictly a product of my imagination.

2. The orcas' use of the young dolphin in teaching their young how to kill is imagination on my part. The idea was triggered by a comment made to me by a staff member at Sea World, San Diego. We were discussing the graphically recorded attack of an orca pod on a young blue whale, in 1978. Cliff Tarpy, in "Killer Whale Attack," *National Geographic,* April 1979, pp. 542–45.

The attack was observed from the research vessel *Sea World* off the tip of Baja California. About thirty orcas were attacking a young sixty-foot blue whale, biting away great slabs of flesh as the whale swam slowly along, unable to escape because its flukes had been shredded by the orcas. The researchers followed the whales for five hours, recording the event with movie and still cameras. At about 6:00 P.M., the orcas suddenly broke off the attack and left the area. The severely wounded blue whale continued swimming slowly on, probably to its death.

Sea World scientists later studied and edited the hours of film. According to the staff member's remarks, at least some of the scientists suspect that the adult orcas were using the unfortunate blue whale to teach the pod's juveniles how to kill. The edited version of the film is available for viewing at Sea World, on a restricted basis, I believe.

CHAPTER EIGHT

1. A man who had been a student at the marine biology station in Edmunds, Maine, at the time told me that he had seen humpback whales in the bay near Cobscook Falls. Such behavior appears to be atypical of humpbacks, so I opted for finbacks, which frequently pursue herring among the rocky coastal archipelagos of Maine and the Canadian Maritime Provinces.

2. Among the popular theories regarding this stranding were rumors that an orca was in the area and that the dolphins stranded themselves to escape the orca. Another rumor had it that earth tremors caused the stranding. Some witnesses thought they were committing suicide, but I find this explanation implausible. If the animals were bent on suicide, why did only a third of them strand themselves? It seems more likely that mothers and calves or close friends were trying to stay together or help each other.

3. The human perspective on this stranding, and the events surrounding it, are taken largely from a conversation I had with Inland Warden Ernest Smith. Events narrated from the dolphins' perspective are, of course, purely imaginary.

According to Mr. Smith, the rumors of orcas and earth tremors were never confirmed. He said tremors have never been reported in that area, although he allowed that dolphins might be able to sense such phenomena when people could not. Be that as it may, I see no reason why tremors would make dolphins strand themselves. If anything, earth tremors should cause them to seek open sea.

Lagenorhynchus acutus are rarely seen in that area. According to Smith, they usually venture no farther inshore than Campobello Island. Still, he doubts that they merely became lost and wandered into the cove or that they were frightened there by unknown causes. Rather, he thinks my hypothesis is plausible—that the dolphins had probably hunted successfully there before, when the tide was favorable, and this time simply misjudged the tidal swing.

Smith said the reported shooting was atypical. Most people in his area like dolphins.

4. J. R. Geraci; S. Testaverde; D. J. St. Aubin; and T. Loop, "A Mass Stranding of the Atantic White-Sided Dolphins (Lagenorhynchus acutus): A Study into Pathobiology and Life History," *National Technical Information Service,* Washington, D.C.: Pub. PB289361, 1978.

D. E. Sergeant, "Ecological Aspects of Cetacean Stranding," in *Biology of Marine Mammals: Insights through Strandings,* ed. J. R. Geraci and D. J. Aubin, U.S. Marine Mammal Commission Report MMC-77/13, pp. 94–113.

Chapter Nine

1. I observed these events during a Wings, Inc., expedition over Hydrographer's Canyon, about 80 nautical miles south of Nantucket, in September 1982. Except for Dr. Steven Katona from the College of the Atlantic and another mammalogist whose name escapes me, I was the only "whaler" (as the "birders" called me) aboard. Wings, Inc., had promised me that cetaceans and pelagic birds would receive equal time, but we quickly left astern the spectacular tail-walking spotted dolphins to pursue one white-faced storm petrel. This bird is rarely seen in U.S. continental waters, but so, too, are "dancing" spotted dolphins. I was beside myself, but so greatly outnumbered that my protests had no effect. *Moral:* Never go to sea with "birders" unless the study of birds is your sole reason for going.

2. J. M. Perez; W. W. Dawson; and D. Landau, "Retinal Anatomy of the Bottlenose Dolphin *(Tursiops truncatus),*" *Cetology,* No. 11, December 31, 1972. The authors found that *Tursiops* has a duplex retina (i.e., containing two types of photoceptors—rods and cones) in which cones are by no means rare. This suggests functional color discrimination. The paper cites other research by Mann (1946) showing that cones are also present in the retinas of sperm whales *(Physeter catadon)* and fin whales *(Balaenoptera physalus).* These findings dispute the widely held belief that cetaceans are color-blind.

Another case for color perception in *L. Acutus* is the presence of bright yellow flank stripes, which are visible from considerable distances when the animals leap above the surface. Such color patches appear to serve no useful camouflage purpose; therefore, they are probably perceptible to the animals, perhaps enabling them to recognize others of their species as they breach.

AFTERWORD

1. J. Bastian, "The Transmission of Arbitrary Environmental Information Between Bottlenose Dolphins," in *Animal Sonar Systems—Biology and Bionics*, Vol. 11, ed. R.-G. Busnel (Jouy-en-Josas 78, France: Laboratoire de Physiologie Acoustique, 1966), pp. 803–73. Bastian concluded that one dolphin, presented with a flashing or steady light, could "tell" another dolphin, partitioned from the first, to push one or the other of two paddles.

J. Bastian; C. Wall; and C. L. Anderson, *Further Investigation of the Transmission of Arbitrary Information Between Bottlenose Dolphins*, Naval Undersea Center, Technical Publication #109, 1968, 40 pp. This paper concluded that the dolphins responded to self-taught cues but had no comprehension of the nature of the task.

2. R.-G. Busnel and A. Classe, *Whistled Languages* (Berlin, Heidelberg, New York: Springer-Verlag, 1976) English edition, p. 98.

3. Sterling Bunnell, "The Evolution of Cetacean Intelligence," in *Mind in the Waters*, ed. Joan McIntyre (New York: Scribners, 1974), p. 58. Also see marginal note by Peter Warshall.

4. Sheri Lynn Gish at the National Zoological Park, Washington, D.C., recorded over one hundred hours of spontaneous exchanges between dolphins in visually isolated, acoustically linked tanks. Patterns of exchange emerged: communicating dolphins rarely interrupted each other; they tended to match exchanges (whistle-whistle, click-click); they exchanged short vocalizations rapidly, paused longer between longer ones. Conclusion: definite interaction with specific patterns. Is it language? Too early to tell.

5. D. W. Batteau and P. R. Markey, *Final Report*, China Lake, Calif.: U.S. Naval Ordnance Test Station, Contract N00123-67-C-1103 (1967).

6. L. M. Herman, ed., *Cetacean Behavior: Mechanisms and Functions* (New York: Wiley, 1980).

Index of Other Sea Creatures

breaching of, 19–21,
99–100
feeding habits of, 67–70,
81, 87, 94–95, 188 n.1
migration of, 158, 160,
163–64
Puck, 80–84, 158,
187 n.5

Killer whale. *See* Orca
Kittiwake, 14, 26
Krill, 93–95, 188 n.1

Mackerel, 17, 29, 30, 43–44,
104–05, 166–67
Mackerel shark, 139–40. *See
also* Porbeagle
Mako shark, 25–26, 61
Minke whale, 18–20, 65,
66–67, 94, 145

Orca, 34, 36, 40–41, 184 n.5,
184 n.6, 192 n.2
attacks by, 72–79, 130–38,
140–43, 191–92 n.2

Petrel, 95, 193 n.1.
Pilot whale, 51, 145, 167–68,
184 n.5, 186 n.2
hunting habits of, 37–39,
155, 164–67, 186 n.5
Porbeagle, 139–40, 156
Puck (humpback whale
individual), 80–84, 86,
158, 187–88 n.5

Right whale, 20, 49–51,
119

Seal, 54, 72. *See also* Harbor
seal
Shark, 5–6, 22–23, 25–26,
34, 62–63, 97–99. *See also
under names of shark
species*
Shearwater, greater, 95–97
Shrimp, 93–94. *See also* Krill
Sperm whale, 31–33,
167–69, 174, 186 n.5,
193 n.2
Squid, 38–39, 71, 160–61,
165–68, 186 n.4
Sunfish, 60–61, 187 n.5
Swordfish, broadbill, 13–
15

Tuna, bluefin, 63–64, 65–66,
74–77, 79, 130–37
Tuna, yellowfin, 41

Whale, 15, 18–21, 31–33,
37–39, 49–51, 63, 64,
65, 66–71, 80–92,
94–95, 128, 139
breaching of, 19–21,
99–100, 102
preservation of, 50–51, 84,
85–86, 188 nn.6–7
*See also under names of
whale species*
Whale shark, 98